Fun with GPS

Donald Cooke

ESRI Press
REDLANDS, CALIFORNIA

ESRI Press, 380 New York Street, Redlands, California 92373-8100

All rights reserved. First edition 2005
10 09 08 07 06 05   1 2 3 4 5 6 7 8 9 10

Printed in the United States of America

Library of Congress Cataloging-in-Publication Data
Cooke, Donald, 1941–
     Fun with GPS / Donald Cooke.—1st ed.
        p.   cm.
     ISBN 1-58948-087-2
     1. Global Positioning System. I. Title.
   G109.5.C645 2005
   910'.285—dc22   2004029575

Ask for ESRI Press titles at your local bookstore or order by calling 1-800-447-9778. You can also shop online at www.esri.com/esripress. Outside the United States, contact your local ESRI distributor.

ESRI Press titles are distributed to the trade by the following:

In North America, South America, Asia, and Australia:
Independent Publishers Group (IPG)
Telephone (United States): 1-800-888-4741
Telephone (international): 312-337-0747
E-mail: frontdesk@ipgbook.com

In the United Kingdom, Europe, and the Middle East:
Transatlantic Publishers Group Ltd.
Telephone: 44 20 8849 8013
Fax: 44 20 8849 5556
E-mail: transatlantic.publishers@regusnet.com

Cover design by Sara Bobbitt
Editing, book design, and book production by Michael J. Hyatt
Print production by Cliff Crabbe

CONTENTS

PREFACE

Tele Atlas maintains the premier street database for business GIS applications in the United States and Canada. GPS is essential to that work.

At Tele Atlas we also use GPS as the centerpiece of our community and educational outreach programs. We conduct a GPS Treasure Hunt when school groups visit our headquarters, or when employees are asked to demonstrate our workplace activities in a classroom. As part of our Community Paid Time Off program, many Tele Atlas employees use our GPS equipment to assist with conservation easement monitoring or to train local residents in recreation trail mapping.

We do this because it's fun and useful, and it reinforces both what students are learning in class and Tele Atlas' role in making our technology relevant and helpful to our community.

Mike Gerling
COO, Tele Atlas, North America

ESRI is committed to improving all aspects of life on our planet through use of geospatial technologies like GIS and GPS.

These technologies are powerful, empowering, and crucial to the viability of long-term survival of endangered species and the wise use of resources to sustain life on earth.

These technologies are also fun. Don's book makes this point, while reminding us that the fun gadget you got as a gift is also a serious research instrument and an irresistible hook to lure today's tech-happy kids into realizing the importance of their studies and applying them to making the world a better place to live.

ESRI is pleased to have some of our tools featured in this publication. Use them to have fun, and perhaps to see a way that you can lend your talents to saving the planet!

Jack Dangermond
President, ESRI

ACKNOWLEDGMENTS

This book wouldn't exist without the support of Mike Gerling, Tele Atlas' COO, and the leap of faith on the part of Jack and Laura Dangermond at ESRI. Mike, many thanks for letting me take the time to put this material together. Jack and Laura, I hope you're pleased; GIS really does put the "fun" into GPS! Laura, I'm still willing to GPS your dogs; just ask!

Fun with GPS contains lots of somewhat arcane material about GPS; I had lots of help digging up the details. Two local teachers, Al Zielinski and John Kitzmuller, served as summer GPS interns with me in the late 1990s; I hope they took away as much from the experience as I learned from them.

My colleague Colleen Stevens taught me a lot, ranging from her teaching style to her willingness to take a soldering iron to a $4,000 GPS unit—which I suppose you have to do occasionally in the process of getting your geophysics PhD using survey-grade GPS along earthquake faults in Indonesia.

The Web makes it possible to shout for help when stuck. Many people responded with ideas, answers, and suggestions: Andy Toepfer and Ned Swanberg at VINS, Marv White and Ken Milnes at SporTVision, Nancy Lambert at the UNH Cooperative Extension, and Val Noronah and Mike Goodchild at UC Santa Barbara all helped me puzzle out speed calculation accuracy issues.

Tim Loesch and Chris Pouliot at the Minnesota Department of Natural Resources patiently answered questions, tested one of my Garmin® Geko™ units, and even introduced a modification to DNR Garmin on my behalf. Ted Gartner and his techies at Garmin compiled answer after answer to various technical and marketing questions. The book would not be possible without these great Garmin products or Minnesota DNR's generous donation of their software to all of us.

My friends at Tele Atlas were wonderfully supportive. Many of the *Fun* topics were suggested by my workmates here. They persuaded their children to wear or carry GPS units, assisted me on school projects, and served as subjects for various mini-chapters. One even presented me with a *fait accompli* topic; I only had to take a couple of photos!

Many thanks to all the participants—friends, neighbors, and innocent bystanders alike—who agreed to try out the various *Fun* projects. Very few people said no to the bearded stranger asking if he could duct-tape some wires to their jacket or attach an antenna to their collar or helmet. More than a hundred people participated directly one way or another in getting my GPSs to move around on or above the surface of the earth. Still more people worked behind the scenes: Vickie French did a superb job tracking down model releases for two boatloads of rowers. Adena Schutzberg provided counsel, advice, and ideas. And Keith Merrick is the only pilot I know who would take me up in his airplane on short notice for a mission with untested consequences.

Also, thanks to Lockheed Martin Space Systems Company for permission to use the artist's rendering of a Block IIR GPS satellite that appears on the cover, title page, and page 98.

I learned a lot about publishing from my neighbor Ed Gray (*graybooks.net*) and the folks at ESRI Press: Christian Harder, Judy Hawkins, and Michael Hyatt. I promise all of you the next one will be easier!

I couldn't have done any of this without help from my family: Emma's photographic talents, Dylan's researching and programming skills, and Abby's nautical competence. Most of all, my wife Jenny was a constant, loving source of inspiration and support throughout the whole process.

INTRODUCTION

I've been interested in electronic positioning and navigation ever since the early 1980s when a friend invited me to crew in an overnight sailboat race, adding that he had installed a new LORAN receiver and could I figure out how to run it?

Now GPS has supplanted LORAN, and tiny units costing just over $100 can locate you with car-length accuracy. These GPS units are irresistible to gadget lovers, and make great gifts.

But what do you do with your new GPS? If you're a fisherman or hunter, it becomes part of your kit, but what about the rest of us? Once you've found the geocaches within driving distance of your home, what do you do?

This dilemma rises from a simple fact: if you only have a GPS, you're only having half the fun. It's like you've got front-row seats at the big game but you head for the exits during the half-time show. Most of the fun with GPS comes from the ability to make maps of locations you've stored in your GPS memory.

Because I've worked in digital mapping since 1966, I took this for granted. I always had access to the best GIS (geographic information system) software available, and I found myself routinely mapping GPS data I had gathered or that came out of various school and community projects.

I took GPS units everywhere I went and recorded airline flights, cross-country ski treks, and driving trips. I was having fun, and wanted to share the fun with others. Then, thanks to ESRI and the Minnesota Department of Natural Resources, it became possible for anyone with a PC and an Internet connection to map GPS data with free software! That's what triggered the idea for this book.

Your GPS is a miracle of modern technology; it ranks right up there with the Internet in the pantheon of useful spin-offs of military technology. So have fun! And share the fun with your students, friends, and community.

Donald Cooke

If you're browsing through this book, and want to get into the world of *Fun with GPS,* here are some guidelines for avoiding disappointment:

1 *Fun with GPS* is based on mapping tracks stored in your GPS.

2 To do the activities in the book, you'll need a computer, a printer, and an Internet connection. Apple® Macintosh® users will be frustrated, because the software I describe runs only on Microsoft® Windows®. If you're from Macintosh Nation, see *www.gpsy.com* or *macgpspro.com.*

3 In order to map data, you have to download it from the GPS memory. You will need a special cable for this purpose. While this isn't very expensive, your GPS must have a port on it for the cable! Put this on the "must have" list when shopping for your GPS.

4 The examples in this book are heavily slanted to GPS units made by the Garmin company. The overriding reason is that Garmin GPSs can be set to record track log positions at fixed time intervals, for example, one point per second. At present, you can't do this with Magellan® GPSs. I doubt that it would be difficult for Magellan to change this, and I've recommended to them that they do so. Consequently, if you own a Magellan GPS you're not going to be able to re-create many of the examples I show in the book.

5 GPS units with Wide Area Augmentation System (WAAS) capability are twice as accurate as units without WAAS. Most new GPS units are WAAS-capable, but put this on your checklist also.

6 Some of the examples I show will only work well with a Garmin 76, because it stores track points with more precision than other models.

Take a close look at the Garmin GPSMAP® 76, which will store 10,000 track points compared with the 2,048 stored by the plain 76 model. You can also attach an external antenna to the Garmin 76.

Using your GPS

Every spot on the earth, no matter how small, has a unique location denoted by latitude and longitude. Latitude measures how far above or below the equator you are. Longitude tells how far around the earth you are from Greenwich, England. Your GPS (global positioning system) device determines latitude and longitude down to about 10 feet.

Every GPS unit has a radio receiver that's tuned to pick up very faint timing signals broadcast continuously by a constellation of satellites orbiting far overhead, fifty times more distant than the normal path of the space shuttle. Your unit has a powerful computer that processes those timing signals to calculate your latitude/longitude location every second. GPSs have data screens that can display location or calculated direction and distance to your destination, as well as several buttons that let you select operational features.

Many GPSs have extra memory installed so you can upload map data through a cable attached to a personal computer. This lets the GPS show where you are relative to streets, towns, or nautical navigation aids, rather than just announcing that you are at N 43.57463, W 72.28475 and letting you puzzle it out.

Most GPSs will let you store and label five hundred waypoints and navigate to them along a route you can define and store. GPSs also quietly keep track of where you've been and give you ways to retrace your route.

All of this is described in the manual that came with the GPS. It's not my purpose to reiterate this information, although the rest of this chapter will give you some tips to make your GPS work to its potential and illustrate some fun things you can do with it just as it came out of the box.

I hope you enjoy these chapter 1 activities. But they're not what this book is about. Later on I'm going to tell you much more about that last GPS function I mentioned: your GPS's track log. You can control how track points are saved, and use free or inexpensive software to download these points to your computer and map where you've been.

But I'm getting ahead of myself; read on!

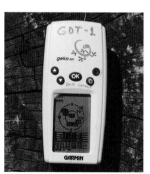

Good practice with GPS

- Let your GPS wake up before each use. Turn your unit on and leave it undisturbed where it can see open sky for a few minutes. It needs to record the ephemeris (orbital parameters) for any satellite it might use to locate you. The ephemeris message takes thirty-seven seconds to transmit and your GPS must start over if its view of any satellite is blocked and the message is interrupted. If you're walking under trees, your GPS won't be able to collect these messages. If it doesn't have the ephemeris for a given satellite, it can't use it in your location solution, meaning reduced accuracy or no reading at all.

- Use WAAS (Wide Area Augmentation System) to double the accuracy of your GPS. Your GPS manual will tell you how to turn WAAS on. Unlike all the other GPS satellites, the WAAS "birds" (numbers 35 and 47) are in geosynchronous orbits in the southeast sky if you're on the east coast and the southwest sky if you're out west. (More info is at *gpsinformation .net/waas/acquire-waas-a.html*.) Make sure your GPS has a clear path to the WAAS satellite during warm-up.

  It can take more than thirty minutes to get WAAS working the first time. After that, it'll happen while your GPS is collecting ephemerides. Most GPSs will show a little "D" in each signal-strength bar, or say "3D Differential" to show that WAAS is working.

- Show due diligence and pay attention to details: fresh batteries, track log set up right, and so on.

- Use common sense: never stake your life on a pair of AA batteries! Remember, if you're hiking and get cold and tired and call 911 to tell a dispatcher your GPS coordinates, they're going to ask you the nature of the emergency. To them, cold and tired isn't an emergency. And your local peace officers won't

be sympathetic if you drive erratically because you're also trying to run your GPS, or if you make an illegal turn because "the GPS told me to turn there."

- Use the Statue of Liberty stance to give your GPS the best chance to receive all available satellites. An external antenna is great if you need both hands free while skiing or hiking.

Hold your GPS up so it has a clear view of the sky. Lady Liberty's GPS is working better than Kokopelli's!

Most GPSs have a screen that shows a sky map and a bar chart of signal strength for each satellite. While the GPS is recording an ephemeris, the bar for that satellite will be gray. Once the ephemeris is stored, the bar turns black. These stored ephemerides* will be valid and usable for about an hour, and your GPS won't need to re-collect them if you lose a satellite in tree cover or behind a building, or even if you turn it off for a short while.

You'll hear me use the term "under good conditions" throughout the book when I'm talking about GPS accuracy. By this I mean WAAS is enabled, ephemerides have been recorded, and the GPS antenna has a clear, unrestricted view of the sky.

---

* I don't know why, but "ephemerides" is the plural of "ephemeris." To sound like an expert, say "ee-FEM-er-is" and "ef-fi-MARE-uh-deez."

Window seat 1

Yes! Your GPS will work fine on an airplane!

It'll tell you where you are, how high you're flying, and how fast you're going. I remember the first time I tried a GPS on a plane, thinking that it wouldn't work at all bottled up inside a huge aluminum tube. I was amazed when my GPS picked up seven, eight, or nine satellites in flight.

Oh yes: request a window seat when you make your reservation. Ask for a row that's not right over the wing. Seven million people request window seats each year; I suspect many of them do so to enjoy the view.

Words of caution: all airlines will require you to shut off your GPS during takeoff and landing. Some airlines, or even individual flight crews, may prohibit their use. So follow instructions, and be sensitive to your fellow passengers if they're nervous about this strange device you're using!

Basic GPSs will tell you where you are only in terms of latitude and longitude. It's up to you to figure out if you're flying over Tennessee or Kentucky, so bring a compact atlas along, and make sure it has a coordinate grid or at least lat/long tick marks along the borders.

Map and book publishers are starting to cater to window-seat fans. For example, check the offerings at *www.spinmaps.com* and Gregory Dicum's new book, *Window Seat: Reading the Landscape from the Air.*

Before you take off, check your probable route on a map and pick out points of interest to look for. Niagara Falls, Shiprock Peak in New Mexico, and Meteor Crater in Arizona are some of the natural features I've spotted. Ski areas, airports, and stadiums are easy to identify.

Remember that if you're flying at 39,000 feet, you're 8 miles up and the nearest thing you'll be able to see will be about 5 miles away from the flight path. It's frustrating to fly right over something interesting and never see it.

Clouds or no clouds, the most basic GPS can tell you where you are.

A basic GPS will tell you your latitude and longitude and display point locations of some larger cities. The next model up usually includes much more detailed internal map information; see above. Note how closely these two units agree on speed, altitude, and distance to Detroit.

Geocaching

Geocaching is an outdoor game involving finding a hidden "cache" of treasures identified by latitude and longitude.

My wife Jennifer and I tried geocaching with friends in Florida last January (see "Shelling on North Captiva," page 74). We chose a cache from *www.geocaching.com* by entering the ZIP Code for Sanibel. The Web site returned a list of caches with those closest to Sanibel on top. We picked a cache near Bowman's Beach, a family favorite, and printed out the information for it. I set up a Garmin 76 GPS for Jenny by entering the cache's coordinates as a waypoint, then activating the GPS's "Go To" function.

Easy? I suppose so—if you're a crow and can travel in a straight line. The GPS showed the cache just .4 miles from our car. So why did we walk so far? Because we're not crows! The GPS led us to within an eighth of a mile of the site, which was across a large body of water. We had to backtrack and start over but found the site easily enough.

This was a great demonstration that having a GPS doesn't guarantee flawless route guidance. There's a lot more to navigation than simply knowing where you are and the coordinates of your destination. GPS can help with navigation, but you also need a map showing details of one-way streets and turn restrictions for true route guidance.

Web sites
www.geocaching.com
www.navicache.com
www.brillig.com//geocaching

GEOCACHING.COM

Treasure!

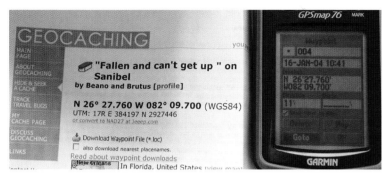

Here's how I entered our cache's coordinates in my GPS. You'll see that *geocaching.com* supplies coordinates in degrees and decimal minutes. Though I like to use plain decimal degrees (nn.nnnnn), I reset the Garmin unit's coordinate display format to degrees and decimal minutes to simplify our geocaching expedition. This doesn't change how my GPS stores the coordinates, just how they look on the display screen.

Tips for geocaching

GPS basics for geocaching: The *geocaching.com* Web site provides coordinates for the cache. Enter these as a waypoint. For most GPSs, you do this by storing a waypoint for wherever you are, then editing its coordinates to equal those supplied for the cache. Once you've stored the waypoint, use the GPS "Nav" or "Go To" function and the GPS will show you direction and distance to the cache.

Don't be frustrated if your GPS shows you're at the right coordinates but you find no cache. Look around a bit. Remember that your WAAS-equipped GPS has a 10-foot error under ideal conditions, and the person setting up the cache may have had an older (pre-WAAS) GPS or perhaps wasn't quite as savvy a GPS operator as you are.

Good GPS stance!

Undocumented feature

Do you want really accurate coordinates for a geocache you're creating? Here's an undocumented feature in the Garmin 76 series: when the waypoint screen appears, press the Menu button. This reveals a screen that allows you to average coordinates for the waypoint for greater accuracy. Try this out!

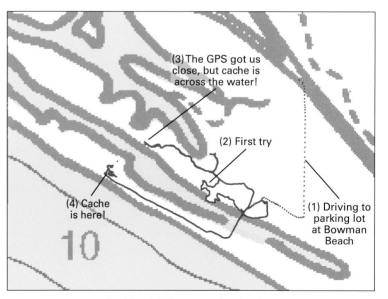

(3) The GPS got us close, but cache is across the water!

(2) First try

(1) Driving to parking lot at Bowman Beach

(4) Cache is here!

10

Track log plot of our geocache adventure

Reports from practically nowhere

In 1959, John Sack wrote a charming book called *Report from Practically Nowhere,* which described his travels to thirteen tiny countries best known to stamp collectors: Lundy, Sark, Swat, and the like.

GPS has revised and updated this notion with the concept of *degree confluences:* places where latitude and longitude both come out even, with no minutes, seconds, or decimal places allowed.

Latitude has a value of zero at the equator and increases to 90 degrees at the North and South Poles. Ignoring the poles for the moment, this means there are 179 *parallels* of latitude (the equator is one of these), each of which has an even number of degrees (43.00000). The same can be said of the 360 *meridians* of longitude; if you walk north or south along any of these, your GPS will show a number with zeros to the right of the decimal point (72.00000).

Parallels and meridians intersect in lots of places, 64,440 to be precise, plus the two poles. A total of 14,027 confluences are on land and more than 10,000 of these have never been visited. Is there anything special at these points? Take your GPS and go find out!

There's an organization called the Degree Confluence Project that's devoted to this idea. Check it out at *www.confluence.org.*

Has anybody been to a confluence point near where you live? Are there any nearby points that haven't been discovered? You could be the first person to log a confluence visit, but you'll probably need your passport and an airline ticket to do so.

After a morning GPSing visitors at the Montshire Museum Science Park (page 104), I resolved to visit a nearby confluence on my way home. At *www.confluence.org,* I found one near a state highway just north of where I live.

So what's there? Hmmm... Looks like generic New England woods. But the GPS doesn't lie! I was there! Honest!

Some confluences are much more interesting. Check out the ones on Antarctica. Admire Dave Brooks' fortitude in tagging N 21, W 157. Visit an apple orchard at N 43, E 2; an Indian village at N 29, E 77; a rice paddy at N 29, E 110. And help out with the ten-thousand-plus remaining confluences!

An interim speedometer

Denis Demers is a car guy who works with me at Tele Atlas. Last summer he hooked a T5 transmission to the 289 Ford V8 in my 1959 AC. We're still working on one problem: finding the right cable to go between the T5 tranny and the old original speedometer. GPS provides an interim solution: I bought a mounting bracket from GPS-Geek on eBay®, and set up one of the display screens on my Garmin eTrex® unit to show speed and time in the largest size. Now I just have to remember to turn the GPS on when I take the car out. The GPS's odometer function is useful too, as the gas gauge is sometimes flaky.

Take your GPS out for a ride. (Get someone else to drive so you can concentrate!) If the speedometer says 50 mph and the GPS says 48.6, who's right? The short answer is the GPS. I'll get back to this issue later, but if you're impatient, type "GPS speed accuracy" in a Web search engine. I just did this and got 8,770 hits; make a sandwich before you start reading.

Denis nearing completion of the transmission swap.

Denis road tests the eTrex speedometer.

My AC meets a cousin at the Mount Equinox (Vermont) Hillclimb. Only 732 ACs were made between 1953 and 1962; such meetings are rare.

Introduction to mapping

Here's where the fun comes in. Take your GPS with you on a driving trip. Bring it along on your boat. Carry it when you go running or cross-country skiing. Attach it to your dog.

Now, if you've set up your GPS right, you'll to be able to download the stored locations of your unit's track to your computer and make a map using free software.

This chapter describes these three steps: how to set up your GPS's track log, how to obtain and use software that will allow you to retrieve stored coordinates, and how to obtain and start using the free ArcExplorer™ GIS data viewer.

There's a lot of material to cover in order to get a great map of your GPS data. I'm not going to be able to explain every step in this little book. If you have some experience with GIS (geographic information systems), then replicating my examples will be easy. If you're learning computer mapping, there are plenty of useful texts to supplement *Fun with GPS.* Two good books from ESRI Press are *Getting to Know ArcView GIS* and *GIS for Everyone.* The latter includes a copy of ArcExplorer and lots of data. *Mapping Our World,* though more expensive, comes with a one-year ArcView® GIS license.

I used ArcView GIS 3.3 software to do the technical stuff. That means some of the menu choices I refer to may be different than those in your version of ArcView. If you have trouble following my steps, you may want to ask a more experienced ArcView user for help. For details about how I did things, consult this book's companion Web site at *www.funwithgps.com.*

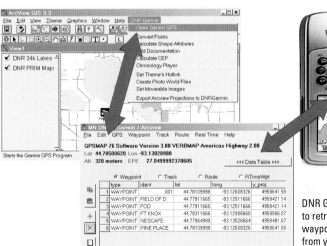

DNR Garmin is the key to retrieving stored waypoints and tracks from your Garmin GPS unit and storing them in the shapefile format used by ArcExplorer and ArcView.

Recording tracks and points

Your GPS can store locations in two fundamental ways: tracks and waypoints. Most GPSs have room for 500 or 1,000 waypoints. Your instruction manual will tell you how to store a waypoint; usually you just press and hold one of the buttons until a waypoint screen appears. The GPS will assign a unique number to the waypoint. Many let you edit this number and change it to an alphanumeric name. My travel GPS contains waypoints I've gathered at various airports. These are more useful and accurate for the Go To navigation function when flying than the name of the airport's city, which may be many miles away.

I find I don't use waypoints very much. In contrast, all of the mapping examples in this book use the track log function. Many GPSs store 2,000 track points. Some store a lot more: my Geko 201, Foretrex™, and GPSMAP 76 units all store 10,000 points.

If you turn on track logging (see your manual), the GPS will start storing track points automatically as soon as it can compute your location. So how does your GPS decide when to store a track point? There are usually three ways for it to do this.

When your GPS is new it is configured to choose track points automatically. If you're hiking slowly on a winding path, it stores lots of points. If you're driving fast along a straight highway, it may store only one point per mile. The default "auto" algorithm usually produces track logs that satisfy most uses.

There are other ways to control track log storage. Besides the "auto" option, Garmin handhelds let you collect track points based on time or distance. You can set your Garmin unit to collect points at whatever time interval you like, down to one second apart. You can also set it to store a track point only if it moves more than a certain distance you specify (in feet on my Gekos and in hundredths of a mile on my Garmin 76 units). Magellan handhelds and Garmin units designed for in-car use don't have the "time" option.

I always choose the "time" method, and I set the time interval to collect as many points as possible, given the size of the track memory and the duration of the trip or event I'm recording. The following is an example of how I think about setting up the track log.

I'm flying from New Hampshire to California. I'll be in the air about 6 hours. I have a Garmin 76 that can save 2,048 track points. Six hours is 360 minutes, or 21,600 seconds. I'm a good citizen so I'll turn the GPS off during ascent and landing. I'll actually be running the GPS for less than 6 hours.

In this case I set the track log to record a point every 10 seconds; with this setting I'm good for about 5 hours and 40 minutes, a safe bet. While I'm in California, I download the points and erase the "active" track log to prepare for the trip home.

Okay, I know what you're thinking. Why doesn't Don save the track log? He can do that ten times and save more than 20,000 points! Right? Wrong! When you save a track log, the 2,000 carefully chosen points get generalized down to about 150 key points. For mapping and speed calculation, you'll want all those little points.

I used GPS for years before it dawned on me how powerful and useful the track log function is. I tell kids it's like the GPS is laying down a trail of breadcrumbs every second wherever they go. If they stand still, the crumbs heap up around their shoes. If they move fast, the trail spreads thin across the landscape.

When you hike slowly along a winding path, your new GPS unit's default "auto" option stores many track points.

When you speed along a straight highway, your new unit stores maybe a point a mile.

DNR Garmin

You've set up your GPS's track log parameters and you've taken it for a ride out in the world. You're ready to make a map. Your track log screen shows that your unit is 90 percent full. You're comfortable that this make sense considering your track log settings and how long you had the GPS turned on. Now you need to get the coordinates out of the GPS and into your computer.

Garmin users' best bet is to download the free DNR Garmin program.* The Minnesota Department of Natural Resources (DNR) has very generously made this program available at no cost. GIS Specialist Chris Pouliot and his boss Tim Loesch have done us all a great service by providing this program.

I can never remember the Minnesota DNR's Web address, so I usually type "DNR Garmin" into a search engine and up it pops. Chris and Tim keep updating the program, and version 4.4 was released in September 2004. If you're running Windows NT®, Windows® 2000, or Windows® XP, get version 4.4 for its great new coordinate projection capabilities. If you're still on Windows® 98, you'll have to use version 4.0.

As the DNR Web site explains, the DNR Garmin program actually is two companion programs. One works as an ArcView extension; for the moment we'll concentrate on the stand-alone mode.

Download and install the program, attach your Garmin unit to the serial port, turn on the GPS, and start the program. If you're lucky, the program will recognize your GPS and you'll be able to retrieve your points. If the program complains that it can't see your GPS, there are two quick things to check.

On your GPS, go to the main menu and to the "setup" and "interface" screens within that. You'll find a place to choose "I/O format" (Geko) or "serial data format" (eTrex). Set this to Garmin. If you're using an eTrex or Geko, make sure the cable connection is firm at the GPS end; it's prone to coming loose.

In the DNR Garmin program itself, on the GPS menu, click Assign Port and ensure that you've assigned the correct port

* Magellan users, try the GPS2GIS program from Steve Foster at *www.arcprogramming.com.* Thank you, Steve!

number. My desktop machine has two serial ports, and it's always an adventure to select the proper one.

Once everything's configured right, the DNR Garmin program will recognize which GPS it's hooked to and announce that it's connected.

Now's the time to download your track log. Click Track and then Download; the data will stream into your computer. Once this is done, click GPS followed by Close Port and turn off the power on your GPS, since the track points are now in the program's working memory.

At this point, click File, then click Save To, then File. . . and navigate to where you want to store your track points using the Windows Save As dialog.

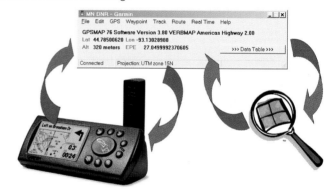

I recommend that you save the track log in at least two of the available formats. First save it as Text File (Comma delimited). Doing this will give you the most flexibility in the future. Then also save the file as ArcView Shapefile (unprojected), perhaps with the same name as your text file. Do this twice, once as lines and again as points. The DNR Garmin program will ask you which you want. You'll need different names for your point and line shapefiles so that the second one you save won't overwrite the first.

DNR Garmin (continued)

You'll be able to load these shapefiles directly into ArcExplorer or ArcView. I usually find the point shapefile most useful, as I can color each point according to its elevation or speed. The line format unfortunately consists of just one long line that can only be displayed in a single color and line style. See whether you prefer line or point shapefiles for your maps. As you look through the book you'll see that I've sometimes chosen to display the points on top of the line shapefile.

Oh darn . . . I was hoping I could wait until much later to bring up the subject of coordinate projections. How can I cover this in a page? Here goes; try not to get overloaded.

Your GPS will always record your track log "breadcrumbs" in units of latitude and longitude. If you follow the instructions above you'll be able to map the GPS track against a background of street centerlines, county boundaries, or perhaps the land ownership parcels in your town.

Often you'll want to map the track log on an aerial photo or topo map background. I'll cover how to find such background "wallpaper" for your travels in chapter 9. For now you need to know that aerial photos and digitized topo maps are based on projected coordinates. If you will be using ArcView, it provides two ways* to convert your lat/long shapefiles into projected coordinates. But if you're using ArcExplorer, it's important to deal with the projection issue right here in DNR Garmin while you're saving your track points.

It's not hard to set a projection in DNR Garmin. On the File menu, click Set Projection. This opens a techie-looking window. Here's what I do for Vermont:

1 Under Datums, scroll up to and click on NAD83 (this stands for North American Datum of 1983).

2 Under Projections, scroll down and click on Vermont.

3 Click OK at the bottom of the screen.

Having done that, I'll save my track log twice more, as ArcView Shapefile (Projected), in point and line form.

When I use an unprojected lat/long background, I can choose my unprojected point and line files. If I map the track against an aerial photo background, I choose the projected shapefiles. Not too complicated.

How did I know to choose "NAD83" and "Vermont"? Um . . . because I wanted to specify Vermont State Plane coordinates, NAD83, in meters. It's the standard for Vermont GIS data. How did I know that? I found that out from the Vermont Center for Geographic Information Web site. How did I find that site? See chapter 9. If you're always mapping around your home territory, you'll only ever have to deal with this once.

Now the bad news: it's not always so simple. What if I had chosen New Hampshire for my example? In steps 1–3 above, just clicking on New Hampshire instead of Vermont projects my shapefiles to New Hampshire State Plane coordinates, NAD83, in meters. No surprises there. But when I download background data from New Hampshire's "GRANIT" Web site, I find out to my dismay that the New Hampshire standard is to use feet, not meters, for State Plane coordinates. I'm out of luck, if I want to use ArcExplorer. In ArcView, I'll have to use the Projection Wizard to make a projected copy of my track shapefiles, and remember to specify feet as the unit.

Sorry folks. I hate to bring up this projection stuff so early in the book. It's probably the biggest single reason that people's maps get messed up. Don't get discouraged! Browse through the examples in chapters 3–8. They will, I hope, give you the incentive to master projections!

---

* (1) ArcView Projection Wizard. (2) Click View, then Properties, then Projection; set Category to State Plane - 1983; set Type to your state or substate zone. Ensure that Map Units is correct (see Vermont/New Hampshire discussion on this page) and click OK. Then make the shapefile you want to project your active theme, click Theme, then click Convert to Shapefile. ArcView will make a copy of your shapefile and give you the option of creating it in the view's projected coordinate system.

ArcExplorer

You can find out about the free ArcExplorer GIS data viewer at *www.esri.com/software/arcexplorer/index.html.* You can download a copy, though the files are huge. Consider buying *GIS for Everyone,* an ESRI® tutorial that comes with a CD containing ArcExplorer and tons of data.

ArcExplorer™

Big "+" button

Add Theme button

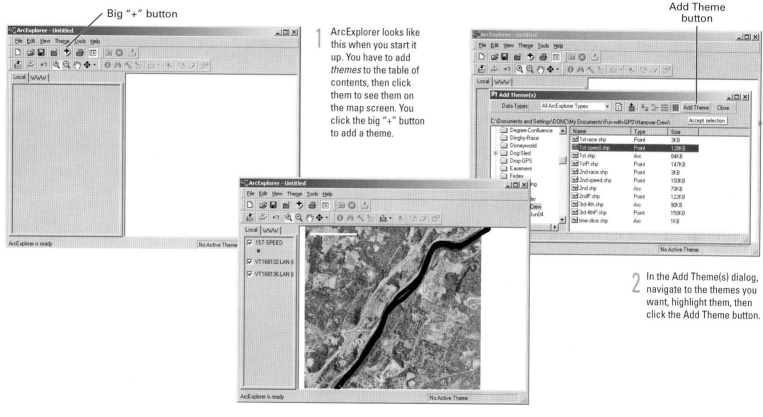

1 ArcExplorer looks like this when you start it up. You have to add *themes* to the table of contents, then click them to see them on the map screen. You click the big "+" button to add a theme.

2 In the Add Theme(s) dialog, navigate to the themes you want, highlight them, then click the Add Theme button.

3 I added the projected point shapefile for Hanover High's Girls 1st Varsity (page 72) and two digital orthophoto quads (aerial photos) for a background.

ArcExplorer (continued)

4 Check 1ST SPEED to make it the active theme, then right-click and select Theme Properties. This dialog lets you control the point symbols. ArcExplorer displays all the track points with size-5, light blue squares.

The river flows from north to south. The track on the right is headed upstream. The boat has stopped for instructions from the coach, and it drifts downstream a bit before taking off to the north again.

5 To indicate speed by symbol color and size, choose Class Breaks instead of Single Symbols and select the MPH field calculated for each point. Now the boat gets a large, dark red symbol when going fast and a small, pale red symbol when going slow. Unfortunately there's no way to get rid of the black border around each symbol. When you zoom out and the symbols pile up on each other, all you see is the black outline. This is a very rudimentary peek at GIS mapping, but you'll see this kind of functionality in most mapping programs.

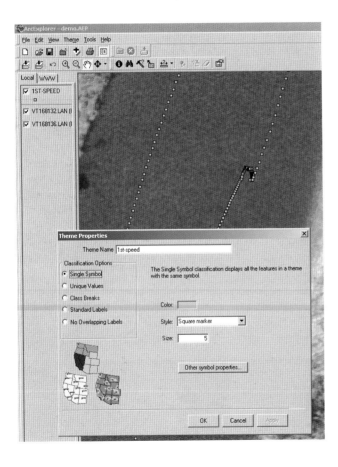

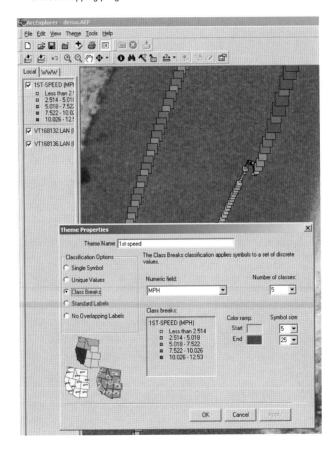

GPS on snow and ice

The *Fun with GPS* story really starts in the frozen North on January 18, 2004. That was the first day I showed up at an event to recruit somebody to carry a GPS for the book.

As you read this book, you'll see that many of the projects are seasonal. I had to wait until spring to GPS most activities, and had just a few weeks of winter to cover the "snow and ice" events. As it happened, the snow melted before I got a chance to GPS my neighbors in the Pinnacle Snowmobile Club. If you run a sled in the winter, write a chapter about it on your own!

I went into this book project feeling that I knew everything I needed about GPS to do the job. After all, I had been experimenting with GPS for a decade, including real-time and post-processed differential, carrier-phase, and testing accuracy at National Oceanic and Atmospheric Administration (NOAA) first-order control points. But as soon as I calculated Thea's skating speed in a race at Lake Morey, I uncovered the issue of precision of coordinates in track logs. Though I was first introduced to this phenomenon in 1968—how many decimal places to allow in representing coordinates—I didn't realize the extent to which it would affect my *Fun* projects.

Three weeks later, I got another surprise. Although I thought I was current on GPS accuracy issues, having been an early tester of the new National Standard for Spatial Data Accuracy (NSSDA) in 1999, I had never encountered the much more slippery issue of relative accuracy of GPS points. By this I mean that one second, your consumer GPS may calculate a location that is actually 3 meters away from the "true" location. Now, what about the point it calculates the next second? Is it likely to be 3 meters away in some other direction? The answer is no. For a lot of reasons, it'll probably be very close to the last reading. This issue turned out to be extremely important to the process of calculating speed from GPS tracks.

More on all of this later in the book; in the meantime, enjoy a GPS winter.

Nordic skating marathon

Two days after basking in the Florida sun (see "Geocaching," page 4, and "Shelling on North Captiva," page 74), I found myself on frozen Lake Morey, Vermont, for a national nordic skating marathon. After a hasty introduction minutes before the start, Thea van der Geest agreed to carry a Geko GPS in her novice warm-up 5K race. As I taped it to her collar, I heard her ask my wife, "What is a GPS, anyway?"

We had to leave before the main event ended but got some pictures anyway.

Thea reported that the 3-ounce Geko didn't add too much to her time.

Close inspection of Thea's track clued me in on a limitation to using Geko and eTrex GPSs. Both units measure location and store track points at a very high precision, but Garmin software for accessing stored track logs clips off some of the precision. You can see how Thea's position seems to jump along checkerboard squares about 2 meters apart instead of following a smoother curve. The map is still useful, but this coordinate clipping wreaks havoc on speed calculations. Details on the phenomenon follow throughout the book.

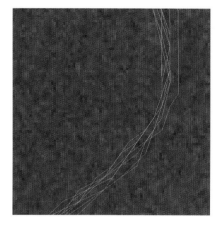

Here's a map of Thea's race. The background orthophoto shows portions of Camp Lanakila, one of Vermont's oldest activity camps.

Sue's backcountry ski trip

Sue McCowan met her husband Guy when she worked at GDT in the 1980s. They're both extraordinary athletes; at GDT Sue regularly gave lunchtime slide shows of her climbing trips to Aconcagua or Uzbekistan.

I asked if she was doing any skiing where she now lives in Colorado, and she agreed to attach a Geko to her pack on a weekend trip along the continental divide.

Sue and Guy rode the Monarch ski lift, but instead of skiing back down they headed north for a day of exploring along the continental divide.

A morning's skiing captured by the Geko. The track log was set to one point every three seconds. Sue's track is color-coded by elevation.

I've bought dozens of nickel-metal-hydride (NiMh) rechargeable batteries for digital cameras and GPSs. For some reason (ignorance?), when I shipped a couple of Gekos out to Sue for this trip, I thought good alkaline batteries would last longer. Well, they didn't.

Sue only got about four hours of tracks each day. This introduced me to the world of charge density and milliamp-hours. As a result of this I started running stress-tests of GPSs outdoors in the cold with various kinds of batteries, and I changed my buying habits to pay a bit more for extra mAH capacity. Pay attention to these numbers.

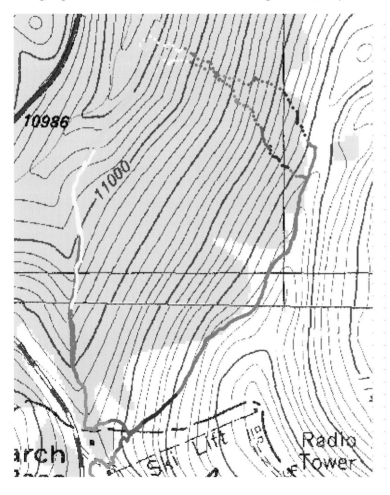

10986

11000

arch

Ski Lift

Radio Tower

This sure isn't New England skiing.

Ice hockey for fun

All too often, ice hockey means $150-per-hour rink fees, twenty minutes spent donning $600 worth of gear, eleven-year-olds being taught how to check, paid referees for games, and five hours sitting in a car every weekend for fifteen minutes of travel-team play. This is fun?

Picture this instead: men, women, and children playing together, no equipment except skates and a stick, lots of sun and fresh air, and no referees, scoreboards, or penalties. No expensive Zamboni at this rink either: everyone pitches in to maintain the ice.

This is still the way hockey is played in some rural New England towns. Could you map pond hockey with GPS?

No organization; no Zamboni; everyone pitches in.

Hexagonal warming hut is a must on icy days.

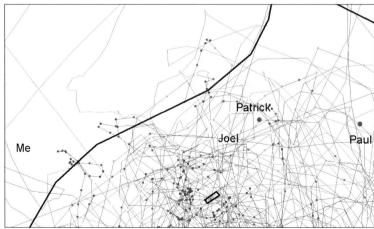

Photo and GPS time stamps allow reconstruction of plays.

Five people played with a Garmin 76 tucked into a pocket and an external antenna duct-taped to a hat or collar.

Track logs were set to record one point per second. Play continued for about forty minutes until the track logs filled. ArcView GIS 3.3 was used for mapping.

Pond hockey takes place over a very small area, about 50 meters square, so a detailed background map is a problem. Even excellent 1:5,000 orthophotos look grainy at this scale. I skated around the playing areas with a Garmin 76 and made a simple outline map for orientation.

There's no penalty box for friendly infractions.

Two rinks, lots of action; this is only five out of fourteen players.

Play until dark. Yes, they do know who's on which side.

Sten and Iver ski for CHaD

The Children's Hospital at Dartmouth (CHaD) holds an annual fund-raising event at the Dartmouth College Skiway. I'm still not sure how the event worked, other than you got points for costumes, face-painting, number of runs skied, and so on.

Sten and Iver, whose dad works at GDT, agreed to carry GPS units for the morning's events.

We used my standard setup: external antenna duct-taped to the helmet, antenna wire taped to an inside clothing layer, Garmin GPSMAP 76 in a pocket recording one track point per second.

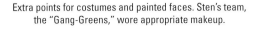
Extra points for costumes and painted faces. Sten's team, the "Gang-Greens," wore appropriate makeup.

Iver warms up his GPS.

Microsoft Excel speed calculations showed ten-year-old Sten going 50.2 mph at one point, and that's just the horizontal component of his motion. Taking into account change in elevation, his speed over the snow was actually much faster than that.

me	Lat-dif	Long-dif	Lat-dif-feet	Long-dif-feet	Dist-feet	Speed-calc
004/02/28-15:41:09	0.00015884	0.00001174	57.9100	3.0900	57.9900	39.5377
004/02/28-15:41:10	0.00015976	0.00002606	58.2400	6.8600	58.6500	39.9846
004/02/28-15:41:11	0.00015515	0.00003906	56.5600	10.2800	57.4900	39.1962
004/02/28-15:41:12	0.00016864	0.00004066	61.4800	10.7000	62.4100	42.5477
004/02/28-15:41:13	0.00017175	0.00004744	62.6100	12.4900	63.8500	43.5310
004/02/28-15:41:14	0.00018960	0.00004417	69.1200	11.6300	70.0900	47.7892
004/02/28-15:41:15	0.00019982	0.00004065	72.8500	10.7000	73.6300	50.2004
004/02/28-15:41:16	0.00018817	0.00004610	68.6000	12.1300	69.6700	47.4978
004/02/28-15:41:17	0.00015851	0.00007494	57.7900	19.7200	61.0600	41.6313
004/02/28-15:41:18	0.00016646	0.00006605	60.6900	17.3800	63.1300	43.0397
004/02/28-15:41:19	0.00019404	0.00005289	70.7400	13.9200	72.1000	49.1558

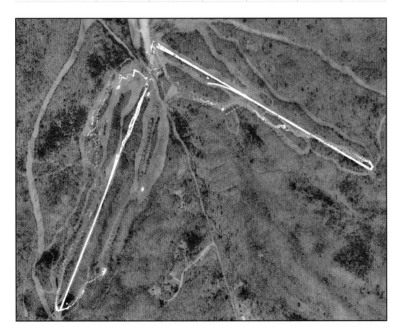

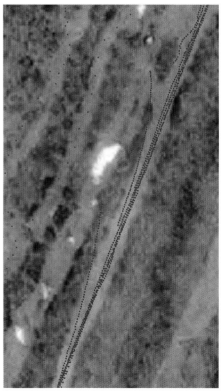

Iver's track on the ski lift, moving from top to bottom of the display. Note the two offshoots from the GPS track; the GPS lost lock on the lift, then regained a position and smoothed locations as it refined them.

Heliskiing

Work colleagues Wayne St. Jacque and Paul Brown volunteered to carry GPSs while heliskiing at Snowbird in Utah. We thought the combination of the ski and helicopter tracks plus the spectacular terrain would provide interesting material. We weren't disappointed! Wayne and Paul taped external antennas to their helmets and tucked Garmin GPSMAP 76 units, set to record one track point every two seconds, into their packs.

The open terrain yielded excellent skiing tracks, but the helicopter traces demonstrated discontinuities and jumps. What was causing that?

While I don't know for sure, I might blame "multipath" for some of these effects: out in the open, your GPS receives strong signals from a particular satellite. It may also receive weaker copies of the same signal reflected off the side of a building, mountain, or snowfield. Normally, the receiver processes only the stronger direct signal and computes a good result.

Now picture what happens inside a helicopter. Its aluminum roof may totally cut off the direct satellite signal, but the Plexiglas® windows may let in a reflection of that signal strong enough for the GPS to process. The reflection will have traveled farther than the direct signal, but the GPS computer doesn't know this and produces a location hundreds of feet away from "true." I bet this accounts for some of the glitches in the helicopter tracks.

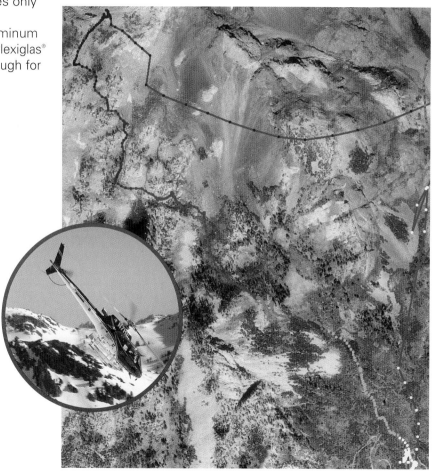

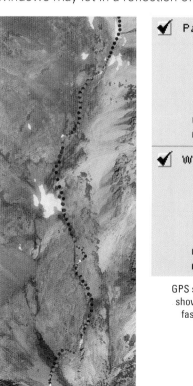

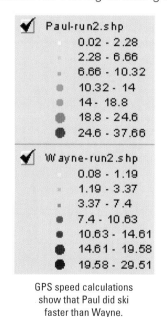

Paul-run2.shp
0.02 - 2.28
2.28 - 6.66
6.66 - 10.32
10.32 - 14
14 - 18.8
18.8 - 24.6
24.6 - 37.66

Wayne-run2.shp
0.08 - 1.19
1.19 - 3.37
3.37 - 7.4
7.4 - 10.63
10.63 - 14.61
14.61 - 19.58
19.58 - 29.51

GPS speed calculations show that Paul did ski faster than Wayne.

Hank's big race

Hank Plaisted used to work at GDT and is an avid musher. For years he and his wife Fran have raised sled dogs and competed in sled and skijoring races. When Hank was president of the New England Sled Dog Association, he organized a race that ran through our back woods in Lyme, New Hampshire.

Hank was one of the first people I called when I started this book. He quickly signed on and told me to come to the seventy-fifth annual running of the World Dogsled Championships in Laconia, New Hampshire. When I showed up for the third day of competition, Hank was holding first place in the six-dog division by a few seconds. I duct-taped a couple of Garmin 76 units inside his sled. As I was turning them on just before the start, Hank mentioned that when he agreed to the GPS project, he had no idea that it would turn out to be the biggest race of his life! But the course was subzero cold and fast, and Hank predicted that if he and the dogs could turn three-minute miles over the nine-mile course (twenty-seven minutes), he stood a good chance to win.

No problem: 26 minutes and 45 seconds, and a well-earned world championship in the six-dog class for Hank. My duct-tape job was in shambles, but the rugged Garmin 76s kept on ticking.

Fran Plaisted usually wins skijoring races; here she harnesses Hinz for Simon's skijoring trial.

Tracks in the water aren't GPS errors: the course runs over parts of frozen Opechee Bay.

Wannabe spectator eyes the big dogs.

Zamir's first skijoring experience

Speed,MPH	
·	0 - 14
·	14 - 16
·	16 - 18
·	18 - 20
•	20 - 22
•	22 - 24.134

Two Garmin GPSMAP 76 units, track log at one point per second.

Twenty-seven minutes of ice chips in Hank's face

Six below zero; good conditions for these athletes

Nordic duathlon

OK, I had never heard of a duathlon, either.

It's a neat idea: several laps with cross-country skis, then click off the skis and click on skate blades to finish the race on ice.

Quechee, Vermont, is a small year-round residential and resort area. The Quechee Inn, with its fields and proximity to Dewey Pond, furnished a great venue for a duathlon. I recruited Stefan, who had come up from Worcester, Massachusetts, to carry a GPS in the duathlon event.

Cell biologist Stefan Wagner clocked an excellent time with my GPS, even without fancy racing duds.

Duct tape secures Stefan's external antenna wire.

Garmin 76, external antenna, track log setting one point per second.

Competitor Jamie Hess *(www.nordicskater.com)* describes wild skating on frozen lakes and rivers at *members.valley.net/~ice/club/index.html.*

Tom Temple from the Dartmouth College ski team shows how duathlon works: two laps on nordic skis . . .

. . . kick off skis, clip on skate blades . . .

. . . for three laps around the Dewey Pond track.

Sean's Sunday drive

What do you associate with a Sunday drive? Warm summer weather, a picnic, kids in the back of the family sedan, rural scenery, rest and tranquility?

Sean has a different idea: temperature just above zero, biting wind, a Subaru Impreza tricked out for rallying, ice tires all around, and a first-in-class at the Boston Chapter, BMW Car Club of America's ice races on Newfound Lake in New Hampshire.

A record ninety-one people had preregistered for timed laps around a meticulously prepared course when I showed up one Sunday. As a certified car nut, I couldn't turn down a ride with Sean; the full roll cage and five-point harness were reassuring, as was Sean's disciplined driving.

Here's a portion of the map I made and sent to Sean. After I mailed it I got to wondering just how accurate those speed calculations were. Clearly they weren't good to three decimal places, but how good were they? This started me on an odyssey that involved most of my friends who use GPS. There's more about this in "Accuracy" (page 123) at the back of the book.

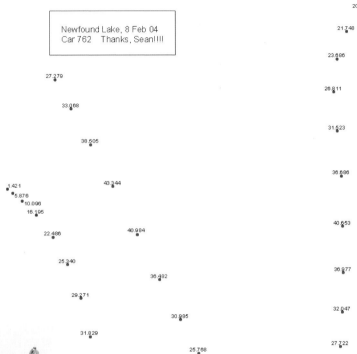

Newfound Lake, 8 Feb 04
Car 762   Thanks, Sean!!!!

Read more about Sean at
www.trunkmonkey.com.

Not your father's snow tires!
Sean's buddy Kris tells how to
make 'em at *www.rallynotes.com*.

Sean starts his run.

This well-driven limo with custom studded tires was quite competitive.

Vintage iceboats

I learned, to my dismay, that iceboats only work on ice . . . and once it snows more than a couple of inches, the season's over. I was about to give up on this minichapter when neighbor Julie O'Hara called one Saturday to report that her family had the boats out on the town pond. Warm weather had melted the snow cover and a cold snap had repaired the ice.

Twenty minutes later I was there with my camera, a couple of GPSMAP 76 units, and a roll of duct tape.

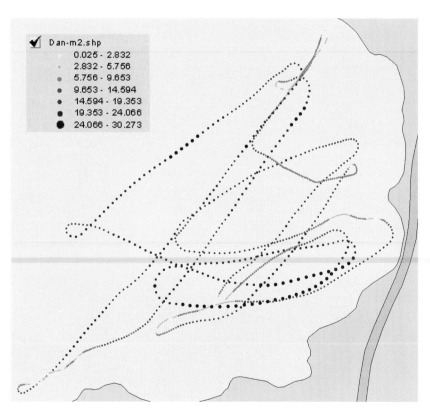

Despite light wind, most of the O'Haras got going more than 30 mph. I turned down Dan's offer to try out one of the boats, in order to get plenty of pictures. This really looks fun!

And the GPS tracks are as pretty as any I've ever captured. I attached a Garmin GPSMAP 76 to each boat, with track log recording at one point per second.

GPS and the animal kingdom

In December 2003, when I approached ESRI founder Jack Dangermond and his wife Laura about this book, Laura immediately asked if we could use GPS to find out where her dogs go during the day. I've never owned dogs, but since that meeting I've been amazed at how many people let their dogs out all day and have no idea where they go.

Could GPS shed light on your pet's travels? Is GPS useful for tracking animals? This chapter gives some examples.

Remember that GPS alone can't find your lost pet. All GPS can do is compute where the animal is and store these locations. Without a radio or cell-phone link, the GPS won't tell anyone where your pet is.

There are pet-finding services, but their technology works on a totally different principle: the pet carries a tiny beacon transmitter that periodically sends out an identifying "chirp." To find the animal, you have to drive around with a direction-finding radio.

There are several reasons why GPS isn't used for pet tracking: (1) GPS is comparatively expensive, (2) you need another system to communicate the pet's location, and (3) GPS is a power-hungry technology, requiring about a hundred times the battery capacity of a beacon.

While working on this chapter, I had a chance to read some of the scientific literature on animal tracking using GPS. Most studies are expensive and arduous, involving netting and tranquilizing wild animals and hoping they can be located months later.*

As the chapter progressed, I recognized that my criteria for selecting subjects were different from those of the scientists. First, I really only wanted to GPS critters who were going to behave reliably and responsibly with my GPS units—mainly so I'd get them back! Second, I hoped they would go somewhere interesting. And finally, I wasn't going to deal with nets and tranquilizer darts. So I ended up with a short chapter.

I really wanted to GPS a sheepdog herding sheep. I've contacted lots of shepherds, but haven't yet found one willing to try. I'm not giving up on this one; check *www.funwithgps.com* to see how I'm doing.

* Type "Macaulay GPS Tracking" into a Web search engine for a good report on tracking various critters.

Hero cruises the Vermont woods

Greg's a science educator. He and I have collaborated on teaching astrophotography and GPS classes; we share a passion for ice hockey. Greg and I were curious about whether we could use consumer GPS for determining the home range of an animal. Greg's dog Hero, named for his hometown on Grand Isle, seemed a likely subject to study.

Greg attached a Geko to Hero's harness and set it up to record a point every three seconds. This setting will fill the GPS's active track log in around eight hours, about the life of two NiMh AAA batteries.

Hero came back from his first day on the job with only ninety-one minutes of data. What happened? There was plenty of battery power left, so we hypothesized that Hero had rolled over and turned off the GPS against a twig or pebble. Greg built a little shield to protect the switch in further tests.

Even with only ninety-one minutes of data, we learned something. Greg noticed that Hero set out immediately for a house where he has a dog friend, and twenty minutes later was a mile north visiting another friend.

Not knowing anything about Hero's social life, I was left to ponder the gaps and discontinuities in Hero's track. Hero was clearly breaking every rule of good practice with GPS, running under trees and rolling over on top of the unit. Both actions make the GPS receiver lose lock. This not only leaves a gap of unrecorded travel, but unleashes a variety of GPS artifacts or "gremlins."

Garmin GPS units have a feature that works well if you're driving and go under a bridge. If the GPS loses lock while moving, it will extrapolate positions at the last computed speed for about half a minute. This is great if you're driving through a short, straight tunnel, but confusing if you're reconstructing a dog's track through the woods.

Try this experiment: Turn on your GPS out in the yard and navigate to a screen that shows speed or preferably speed and position. When the GPS is initialized, it'll tell you you're not moving. Next walk steadily in any direction. Within a second or two, the GPS will display your speed and you'll see the coordinates changing every second. Now stop, and again within a couple of seconds, your speed will go to zero and the coordinate readings will settle down.

Now walk and stop as before, but this time cover the GPS antenna with your hand just as you stop. This will prevent the GPS signals from reaching the receiver, and the GPS will lose lock. You can verify this by checking the signal-strength bars. But for about half a minute, the speed will stay at your walking speed, and the latitude and longitude readings will continue to change, just as if you had kept walking. This GPS feature complicates our analysis of Hero's travels.

Hero agreed to GPS a couple more walks, and both Greg and I noticed a long stretch where Hero walked at a slow, steady pace along a dirt road. What was going on? Later, Greg was introduced to a woman at a meeting totally unrelated to GPS. He recognized her name from a mailbox beyond his house. "Do you live up on Dorchester Road about a mile from where the pavement stops?" (Yes.) "Do you own a dog?" (Yes.) "Were you out walking with the dog last Sunday afternoon?" (Yes.) "Did a young black dog join you for about a mile of your walk?" (Yes.) Mystery solved! The ever-amiable Hero preferred company to darting around in the woods.

Hero's GPS readings in open country are pretty accurate . . .

. . . but loss and regain of signals in wooded areas make tracking less reliable. You can sometimes infer movement based on time stamps on the track points.

In an area with poor GPS reception, any row of equally spaced track points probably indicates Garmin's "extrapolation" feature.

Mapping a chukker

"Chukker" is to polo as "inning" is to baseball. A polo match consists of six chukkers, each seven minutes long. Murray Washburn, who winters his Austin-Healey in our barn, occasionally plays for the Quechee Polo Club. He introduced me to club members who gamely carried Garmin GPSMAP 76 units on their belts, with Gilsson external antennas on their helmets, for a close and hard-fought match with the Yale Polo Club.

"I shouldda learned this by now": I forgot to GPS the field boundaries and the goals. I forgot to record the time each chukker began and ended. So I had to guess where the field boundaries were and pore over the track logs to determine timing. I hope you'll do better!

Patrick Andrew was named All-American and collegiate player of the year while at Cornell in 1989. His right wrist, hit and broken last year by a powerful line drive, seems to have healed perfectly.

Steve Leninski is Quechee's player-coach and captain. External antenna on helmet; GPS in pouch on belt.

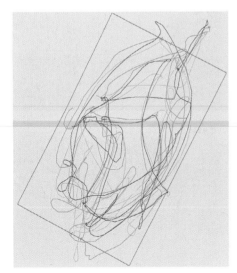

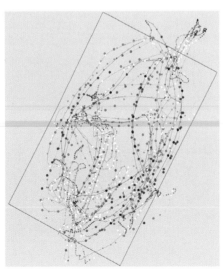

Points, lines, or both? GPS maps don't do justice to the skill and grace exhibited in this sport. I did notice that most players traveled more than 2 kilometers in each seven-minute chukker, with occasional bursts of speed over 30 mph.

Players are always conscious of potential collision danger afforded by thousand-pound animals traveling at up to 40 mph. Veterinarian Charlie Hutchinson IV remounted and continued play following this spill.

Technical note: this polo match was the last event I did for the book, ten days past the manuscript deadline. I was a grizzled veteran of the GPS circuit by this time: everything was going to work; there would be no surprises. So why did Dr. Wira's unit fail to record every fifth or sixth point? And why did Steve Leninsky's do the same thing in the second chukker but work fine in the fifth? I had turned it off and on again in the meantime. Everybody else's GPS behaved normally and didn't lose a single point. All receivers and antennas were mounted in the same manner; a check of my photos didn't show anyone riding around with their head down.

Dale DePriest *(gpsinformation.net)* had warned me about GPS units sometimes being too busy computing to store a track point. It was difficult for me to check the units duct-taped to a belt, especially with the rider astride a horse. I did know they were all running when I retrieved them at the end of the day.

It occurred to me that some of the units might have been operating with the map screen showing instead of the usual start-up screen. Could panning around and redrawing a large active track overburden the GPS's computer? This called for a quick science experiment. Though my five-year-old Camry doesn't look like a polo pony, I could use it to simulate one: use the same two GPSMAP units that misbehaved in the polo game, and the same external antennas, one showing the wake-up screen and the other showing the map zoomed way in. Circle around the parking lot for ten minutes. The map display goes crazy, redrawing, panning, a real workout; no way the processor has time to store all the points. Download the tracks. Nope, no missed points. Garmin says that processor overload is possible, but I couldn't evoke it. Another GPS mystery!

Yale rider (blue helmet) boxed in by cancer researcher Dr. Chuck Wira (left), Charles IV, and Stephane DuRoure.

Stephane (yellow helmet), playing his first game as an American citizen, scored Quechee's first goal. He and his wife Victoria run the highly rated Home Hill Inn and Restaurant in Plainfield, New Hampshire.

Charlie Hutchinson V, just out of high school, was the youngest player by more than a decade.

Mary the Cat helps in the garden

Mary is a good-natured cat who stays close to home. She sleeps in the loft over one of our barns and patrols the garden and nearby fields for mice, chipmunks, and red squirrels. Since she normally wears a collar with bell and ID, she quickly got used to carrying a Geko 201 taped to a small pet harness.

Track points downloaded from eTrex, Geko, and Foretrex GPSs have coordinates truncated to the nearest .001 of a minute (one-sixtieth of a degree). This corresponds to about 2 meters, or 6 feet. Remember, we noticed this in Thea's race (page 16).

While Hero the Dog's range is extensive enough not to be affected by the Geko's coordinate granularity, it really spoils Mary's GPS track.

WARNING Make sure you supervise small animals like Mary if they're carrying GPS units attached to collars, harnesses, or clothing, to ensure that they don't get snagged or strangled by unfamiliar garments and accessories!

Mary's favorite spot: my daughter Emma's shoulder.

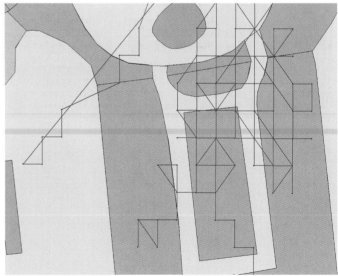

This is the only really unusual background map you'll see in the book. I used an exotic GPS with real-time differential corrections as the basis for compiling this map of our grounds. Other "wallpaper" for GPS tracks is readily available.

In the interests of science and detailed track logs, I tried a couple of different ways to rig a Garmin 76. This model is simply too big for the harness that worked well with the Geko; Mary balked at this rig.

But how about using a remote antenna? Now we're talking! Mary gamely filled the Garmin 76 unit's track log with forty minutes of prowling.

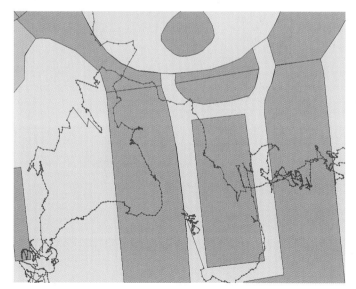

The Garmin 76 track log (red) exhibits fine granularity.

But what does Mary think of carrying the larger GPS? See her letter:

Dear Garmin:

I'm all for GPS and science, but I don't think that the Geko GPS does justice to the subtleties of my perambulations within my home range. My master says that you could change the software either in the Garmin communications protocol or the Geko itself, and people would be able to download active track logs with much more detail than the current one-thousandth of a minute of arc. This would yield Geko tracks with precision similar to that of the larger 76 model. I'm not a large cat, and from my point of view, I would much prefer to carry a Geko than a Garmin 76. I believe I speak for a large number of domestic animals in asking you to make this change.

Yours sincerely,

Mary the Cat

Oops: It might not be so simple, Mary. See page 131.

Squirty's home range

My neighbor Ben Kilham is a gunsmith and wild-animal rehabilitator. You may have seen him on National Geographic and Discovery Channel shows.

Ben pioneered a novel way to raise orphaned or abandoned bear cubs: be a mother bear to them for their first summer, teaching them what to eat, where to travel, and in general, how to be a bear. Conventional wisdom says no contacts with humans; Ben says bears need mothering to be successful in the wild, even if he or his sister Phoebe has to act as the mom.

Squirty weighed only 4 pounds when she came to Ben in 1996. She's an old lady now—a grandmother in fact—and she lives the life of a wild bear in the eastern hills of Lyme. She's shy like most bears—you or I would never see her—but she still lets Ben approach her even if she has cubs or a mate nearby. Best of all, as long as Ben has plenty of jelly beans for her, she's willing to let him attach or retrieve a collar, no tranquilizer darts required.

I called Ben last winter and he was intrigued by my GPS projects. I said that if we could rig a large battery pack, a Geko 201

Ben recycled a battery pack from his "Squirty-cam" video project to power my Geko.

unit set to record one point per minute would gather almost a week's travels. We agreed to try this when Squirty emerged from hibernation. Ben said his gunsmith skills were up to armoring the GPS, and I left it with him along with eight NiMh C cells.

A few weeks later, Ben showed me the collar, and I suggested that he drill a small inspection port so we could ensure that the GPS was turned on. Ben warned that he didn't want to deploy the collar until Squirty sent her three yearling cubs away to fend for themselves. "Those little guys chew on everything; they'll ruin the GPS." Two weeks later I ran into Ben's wife Debbie in the grocery store, and she reported that Ben had put the collar on Squirty. A few days later Ben called; he had the collar back, but the GPS was off. What happened? Low batteries? I hadn't charged them for a month, and NiMh batteries lose 1 percent of their charge each day. Despite the late hour, I drove up to his house in the woods and checked the track log. Fifty-six

percent full! We had lat/longs for 5,600 minutes! I downloaded the track log and ran some quick maps to take to Ben the next morning.

Thursday, June 10, was a big day for the old lady, as shown in the map below. With her mate in tow, she traveled 12.2 miles over her entire home range (red points) in sixteen hours, counting naps and foraging. Thursday night she slept well (blue points); disregarding a few GPS outliers, I don't think she moved for eight hours. Her other days' travels (small green points) include many hours systematically feeding in an area just west of her normal territory (females often expand their range during mating season when protected by the papa bear). Ben quickly went out to determine what food had kept her so interested.

I'm writing this on June 18; Ben picked up the collar at my house this morning and Squirty's probably out making more GPS breadcrumbs already.

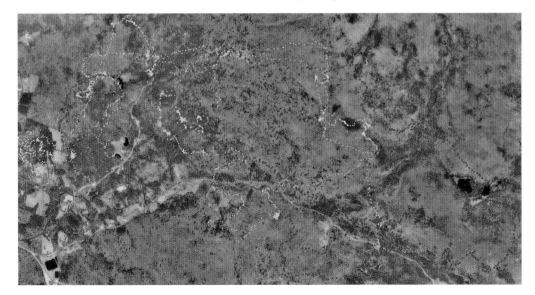

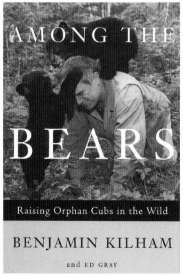

You can read about Ben and Squirty in this book.

GPSing birds

Early in the project I thought it would be interesting to put a GPS on a falcon trained for hunting. I e-mailed Scott McNeff, who instructs at the Equinox School of Falconry in Manchester, Vermont. Scott said that falcons were small and didn't fly far when hunting; had I considered pigeons?

I did a Web search on "GPS pigeon tracking" and found an excellent article on tracking homing pigeons in Germany.* It described how researchers constructed a tiny recording GPS and presented some results of testing pigeons' homing behavior.

The bottom line is that a bird's performance is severely degraded by carrying more than 8 to 10 percent of its body weight. A pigeon weighs about 500 grams, and—alas—my smallest GPS (Geko) weighs 90 grams, or 18 percent of a pigeon's body weight. The German researchers' custom-built GPS weighed 35 grams, and is now available commercially from New Behavior AG in Switzerland.

Web sites   www.newbehavior.com/menu-products/
menu-micro-gps/index_html
www.tauris.de

A surprising amount of research has been done on tracking larger birds such as albatrosses and petrels. Most reports are only available from subscription-only scientific journals; ask a friend at a university. (Thanks, Dylan—"my son the neuroscientist.")

I thought about local possibilities, and came to the conclusion that the larger birds in my area either didn't go anywhere interesting (barnyard geese) or couldn't be relied on to return the GPS (wild turkeys and geese). So no birds; sorry!

* "Homing In with GPS," Karen von Hünerbein and Eckhard Rüter, in *Galileo's World,* summer 2000, www.interbug.com/pigeon/technology/homing_pigeon_with_gps.pdf. The photo of the pigeon, above right, is from this article.

GPS on the road

This is a catch-all chapter: cars, a racing wheelchair, lawn mowers, and a couple of other projects that didn't fit elsewhere. I'll also admit to huge gaps, which you're just going to have to go out and fill in.

1 *Racing lawn mowers.* See *www.letsmow.com.* (Thanks, Johnny Stephens, for this tip!) Go do it!

2 *Bicycles and mountain bikes.* How'd I miss this? Should be easy and rewarding; have fun doing this!

3 *Trains.* A month ago, I was in Baltimore for a meeting and had to get up to New York. I had deliberately and consciously not brought along any GPS or camera gear. Big mistake; I could have tweaked my schedule and tested whether that Acela train really goes 150 mph. I do know from previous GPSing years ago that the regular train hits almost 110 somewhere down in Delaware or Maryland. Lesson learned: never go anywhere without a GPS and camera!

Mapping your commute

In late 2001 I heard that new models in Garmin's eTrex line had WAAS capability. Since it was almost Christmas, and in keeping with the saying that charity begins at home, I bought an eTrex Venture® and got in the habit of leaving it running on the dashboard logging one point per second while I drove to work in the morning. Since my commute is roughly southbound, the east-coast WAAS satellite (number 35) was available in this position.

This wasn't a structured experiment, but was more like a series of observations to see what might reveal itself. Here are a few things I noticed:

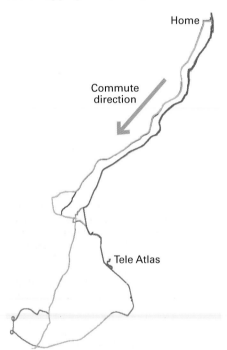

Twenty-eight commute tracks show some variety in route chosen, often determined by the errand of the day. At this scale, only the last track plotted shows in most places.

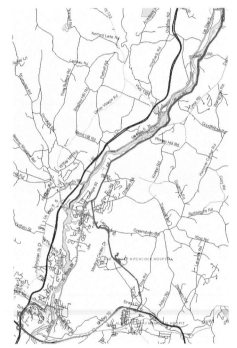

Tracks overlaid on a digital street map are "nominal" in NASA's terminology, or "boring" as my children might say. No surprises. Sometimes boring is good: Tele Atlas makes a living from having streets in the right places.

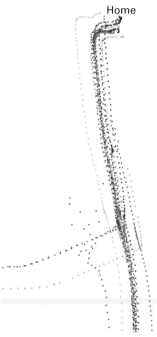

Zooming in was more interesting. Near home, for example, the GPS was "cold" and had to gather ephemerides as I drove along a tree-lined route. At that time I did recognize the importance of waking up a GPS, but wanted to see how the eTrex performed under these conditions. A GPS will start computing positions with as few as three satellites, but these points may be off by tens or hundreds of feet compared with a good fix using as many satellites as possible.

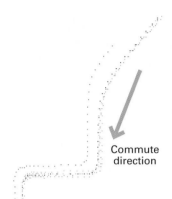

Commute
direction

Here's a phenomenon that jumped out at me.
Coming into Hanover, six routes are bunched
nicely with a spread of about 24 feet. This
might correspond to plus or minus 4 meters
from the centerline—not bad. Then all of
a sudden one track jumps 100 feet off the
road to the west. Possibly the GPS had a
marginal four-satellite fix, then lost contact
with one of these. The GPS will still report
a 2-D fix with three satellites. A 2-D fix is
okay if we don't care about elevation, right?
Wrong! You need a 3-D fix to be confident
of your 2-D (lat/long) location. Without the
fourth satellite, the GPS has to guess at your
elevation when it solves for your location
in space. It can make a pretty good guess
based on something called "height above
ellipsoid," but horizontal accuracy may
suffer. There's no way to know for sure what
happened as I drove along this route, but
it's a good example of why you should be
a savvy and inquisitive user of your GPS,
and in fact of all technology!

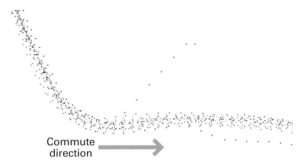

Commute
direction

Uh-oh. What happened here? I'm driving along, staying in my
lane, but the little eTrex shows me zooming 400-plus feet up the
embankment to the northeast. I didn't do this, honest! I didn't
know anything about Garmin's extrapolation algorithm when I first
spotted this. Now, I'm always suspicious of a row of anomalous but
evenly spaced track points. Could the eTrex have lost lock, having
registered its last reading as going off to the northeast? If so, this
is what it might have recorded. We'll never know, but those five
seconds of data have the tell-tale signature of this phenomenon.

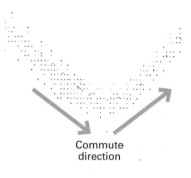

Commute
direction

Here's my left turn at the light to enter the
office park where I work. I can't believe
I never looked at this closely back in
2002. The eTrex's track-log truncation to
.001 minute of arc is clearly revealed by
the grid pattern. I didn't recognize the
impact this has on GPS use for another
two years. If you look closely, you'll see a
few points that aren't snapped to the .001-
minute grid; I had logged my commute
with a Garmin 76 that day. Interestingly, I
wasn't using DNR Garmin in those days;
whatever software I did use clipped the
76 unit's track to an approximately
10-centimeter grid.

Package tracking

In April I had enough material gathered to give a "Know-More-Café" presentation to GDT employees. I described shipping GPS units to various people around the country to record their activities. A coworker, Duane Eppler, approached me afterward and suggested that we ship a running GPS and track its route.

I scoured various shippers' Web sites and consulted with Kelli in GDT's shipping department for regulations on what could or couldn't be shipped. Lots of prohibitions on dead animals, but no mention of operating electronics.

The shipping journey would take about twenty-four hours, several times longer than a Geko's battery life. Out came the tools and soldering iron and soon Geko number 3 was wired to two 11,000-milliamp-hour NiMh D cells—enough power for a week of tracking.

Sue McCowan (see "Sue's backcountry ski trip," page 18) was heading home to Colorado. She agreed to take the Geko home, then start it up, seal the package, and put it in a drop box.

The following afternoon, Geko number 3 arrived still running. I downloaded the track log and took a look. As expected, points showed up along Sue's trip from her office to the drop box. Others plotted at the shipper's transfer facility in Memphis. More showed up at the Manchester, New Hampshire, airport as the package was loaded onto a truck for the drive to Lebanon. There were a few points I deemed spurious: a patch in southern Texas and one out in the Pacific Ocean.

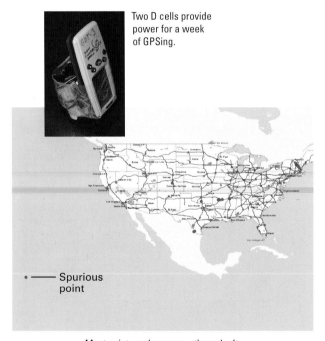

Two D cells provide power for a week of GPSing.

• —— Spurious point

Most points make sense; others don't.

Sue drives the package to the drop box.

2:58 P.M. (Monday)

2:33 A.M. (Tuesday)

The Geko changed planes in Memphis.

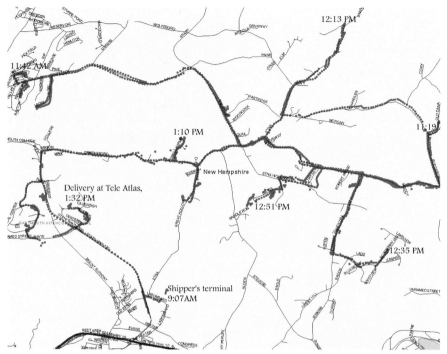

When we zoomed in on GDT's home territory, we got a surprise! GPS time stamps and the shipper's tracking system showed arrival in Lebanon a bit after 9 A.M. We had specified afternoon delivery on the waybill, so our Geko got a tour of Hanover before arriving on time at the office. The delivery vehicle must have had a fiberglass or plastic top to permit such good reception.

Thanks, Duane, Kelli, and Sue!

Manchester, New Hampshire: Geko switches from plane to truck.

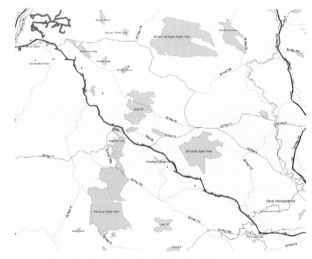

Occasional readings along I-89 to the Lebanon terminal

Bucky's #26 Modified

You met Bucky Demers' dad Denis back on page 8. After years in the top ranks of the NASCAR Pro Stock division, Bucky built an awesome modified that earned him rookie-of-the-year recognition for the 2003 Modified season. I joined the extended Demers family for the first races of the 2004 season.

I let Denis mount the GPSMAP and antenna; I didn't want to take a chance with #26's paint job.

The GPS recorded lots of laps (blue): practice, qualifier, and feature race, plus plenty of cruising at 35 mph under yellow-flag conditions.

Bucky's rooftop door permits more dignified egress than crawling out a window.

Bucky's hotly contested win in the qualifier necessitated remedial bodywork for his car and #76.

Pit area

Even on a one-third-mile track, the modified-class cars turn laps between thirteen and fourteen seconds, and the GPS only logs one point per second. With only thirteen points per lap, my GPS top-speed calculation of 95.8 mph is definitely low since the car is constantly turning and therefore travels farther (and faster) than my straight-line calculations indicate.

Want to know how the pros use GPS in NASCAR? See *www.novatel.com/Documents/Papers/RacingFX%20.pdf.* Author Ken Milnes was very generous with advice and knowledge when I contacted him to help me sort out issues of GPS speed accuracy; thanks, Ken!

Mandi Kehoe, daughter of Bucky's main sponsor, has worked at Bucky's Straightaway Garage after school since eighth grade. She drives her own #26 in the lightning class now.

The powerful #76 car snuck by Bucky to win the feature, but the season's just getting started.

Vintage racers at Lime Rock

I first saw a sports-car race at Lime Rock while still in high school in 1958, and at the time didn't realize it was only the track's second year of operation. I had gotten my license a few months before, and I quickly succumbed to the allure of Lister-Jags, Scarabs, and Porsche RSs.

Almost half a century later, many of these same cars are still running at Lime Rock. The only difference is that they're called "vintage" cars now. Many of them are better maintained and run faster than they did when new.

I took this picture in 1958. The same cars are racing today, but you won't see license plates on many of them. The days of "drive to the track, tape the headlights, race, drive home" are long gone.

My neighbor Peter McLaughlin put me in touch with J.R. Mitchell, whose GMT Racing firm maintains vintage race cars and transports them to racetracks for their owners. I met J.R. at the track at 7 A.M. for the Vintage Sports Car Club of America's "Spring Fling," a low-key event to allow drivers to learn new cars or shake the winter cobwebs out of old ones. I attached Garmin GPSMAP 76 units with external antennas to two cars with track log set to one point per second.

Skip Persson was testing an Alfa Romeo he'd just acquired; remote GPS antenna is taped to the roll bar. Thanks for the great ride, Skip!

Chris Towner was waking up his 1938 Morgan "F" trike from winter hibernation. While far from fastest on the track, this unusual three-wheeler is always a crowd-pleaser, especially when Chris deploys a tiny drag 'chute for the cooling-down lap after the checkered flag.

I GPSed two practices and the late-afternoon race. I've selected one of the trike's practice sessions and, specifically, a section of the track where drivers are setting up for a steep, blind, uphill turn.

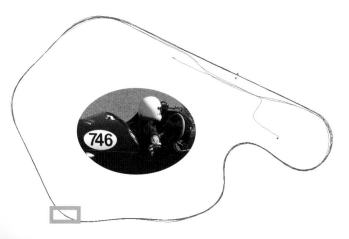

The ArcView Measure tool shows that Chris was very consistent in setting up for this turn, with his two outermost tracks just 4.29 feet apart.

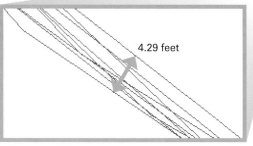

4.29 feet

My impression of Chris has always been that of a conservative, disciplined driver. The GPS log attests to this. His position setting up for this turn mapped out less than 5 feet apart for nine laps over a period of thirteen minutes. This is the combined error of the GPS and the trike's line entering the turn. Great driving, Chris; good work, Garmin. These consumer units are better than most people believe.

Message to outer space

Have you ever tried a corn maze? This is a great moneymaker for small farms with roadside stands—make a maze in a field of corn and charge people to walk through it when they stop in the fall to buy their cider and pumpkins.

Making a corn maze is simple: plant the corn in the spring, and when it has grown ankle-high, mow the maze pattern. The mowed corn won't grow any further, and the remaining corn will form the walls of the maze passageways. The trick is to make a huge pattern accurately, and GPS can help!

For more about corn mazes, see *www.mazeplay.com* and *www.cornfieldmaze.com*. For a great description about using GPS to make the maze, see Franck Boynton's article in the Institute of Navigation's newsletter at *www.ion.org/newsletter/v12n4.html*.

Franck's example used an exotic precision-agriculture GPS, and while I have one of those at GDT, I decided to try the GPS technique using a Garmin 76. Since our back field is planted in alfalfa and hay, I just mowed a huge message in the spring when it was just greening up. The text is "Fun with GPS," of course.

Here's how to think about using GPS for this. Read your GPS manual's instructions about backtracking on your track log. That's basically what I did, backtracking on my old Toro lawn mower.

Before I could backtrack on the "Fun with GPS" message, I needed to get it into the track log. You can do this with Chris and Tim's DNR Garmin program, but that gets into Varsity GIS territory. I'll give you an outline here and you can find more detailed instructions at *www.funwithgps.com*.

While you're mowing, zoom in even farther.

Mowing took just an hour. Garmin 76 duct-taped to a knee; external antenna on hat. Zoom in to 20 or 30 feet and mow along the dotted line.

The secret is to make the message into an ArcView shapefile overlaying a map of the area where you want the message to appear. The map must be in lat/long coordinates, not State Plane or UTM. I used the parcel boundary GIS map for my town.

I started by inserting a "Fun with GPS" label on the map, rotated and sized to the right place. I selected an outline font. Then I made a new line shapefile manually by tracing my label. Finally, I used DNR Garmin to upload this shapefile to the GPS track log.

Sure enough, when I turned on the GPS and went to the map screen, the message was there! I got on the lawn mower and zoomed way in and mowed along the dotted line.

You can't see the message from the ground, so quick, call a friend with a plane! (Thanks, Keith!) The completed book title is 65 feet high and 670 feet wide.

Mary the Cat inspects a serif; a week later the hay would have been too tall to mow.

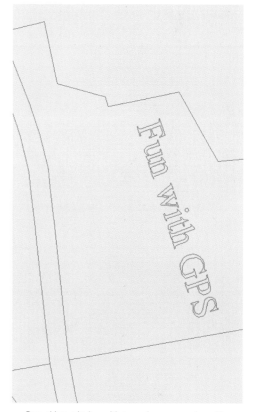

Parcel boundaries with traced message shapefile.

Magic GPS kingdom

Patty O'Neill works down the hall from me at GDT; her boys love Walt Disney World®. She volunteered to take GPSs on her family's fourth visit in as many years. I had just heard of the new Garmin Foretrex model and bought a couple for their vacation. Thomas wore his GPS on his wrist or waist pack. Patty ended up attaching the other high on her shoulder. The differences between their tracks is interesting; it looks like Patty's actually picked up some points inside Space Mountain, an indoor roller coaster.

Garmin Foretrex units, one point every four seconds. Patty is blue, Thomas is red.

Thomas and Goofy; GPS unit is on the pack.

Wish you were here!

The GPS team poses in front of a familiar landmark.

Patty and Thomas wake up their GPSs in the admission line.

Resource

Here's a great resource for GPS users: wonderful aerial imagery for selected cities free for downloading from the USGS "seamless" server at *seamless .usgs.gov*. Georeferenced color aerial photos with 1-foot pixels are posted for forty-seven cities at this writing. More are in the works. The Magic Kingdom is just at the edge of Orlando's coverage; the O'Neills' GPS project was a nice opportunity to showcase this "urban areas high-resolution orthoimagery." Thanks, USGS!

Surprise! The Foretrex picked up signals inside Space Mountain® and three other Tomorrowland® structures. Close zoom showcases fabulous detail in USGS seamless imagery, but also reveals Foretrex coordinate truncation.

Wheelchair marathon

A duathlon (page 28) participant suggested that I GPS the Boston Marathon. I had grown up in Lexington, Massachusetts, where we always had parades and reenactments of the "shot heard 'round the world" battle. Consequently I had never seen this difficult marathon, also held on April 19 and now in its 108th running.

I consulted with runner friends and they warned that nobody facing a 26-mile run would want to carry even a 3-ounce Geko. But somebody suggested the wheelchair event and so I called the Boston Athletic Association (BAA) for a contact.

A very helpful gentleman, Bob Hall, called me and suggested that Tim Kelly, a competitor living in Weymouth, Massachusetts, might be willing to try.

I drove to Weymouth to meet Tim and we worked out where he might mount a Geko GPS on his racing chair. Tim took the GPS out on a practice "push," then sent it back to me to check. The results looked good so I checked out the route for photo sites and shipped the unit back to Tim shortly before race day.

Tim (number 22) leads other chairs in Ashland. Tim's "Team Hall" shirt led me to discover that Bob Hall, who had introduced me to Tim, had been the first wheelchair competitor in the Boston Marathon in 1976. Thank you, Bob!

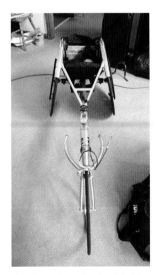

Not your father's wheelchair!

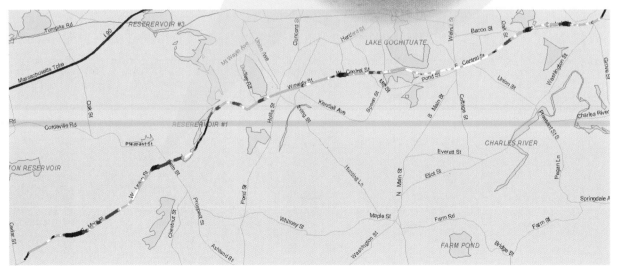

Red is fast, up to 36.6 mph. Blue is slow, painful, uphill work!

Geko 201, tracking
one point per
second, attached
with Mylar® tape.

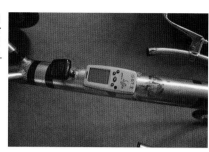

Tim pushes toward
Heartbreak Hill in
Newton.

Tim started the GPS six minutes before his race, and it ran fine for 25 miles. Somehow we ended up missing the last five minutes—about a mile. There was plenty of battery power and track log capacity left. What happened? Perhaps Tim's chair hit a bump that interrupted the battery contacts just long enough to shut off the GPS. We'll never know; I'm just glad this happened a mile from the finish and not a mile after the start!

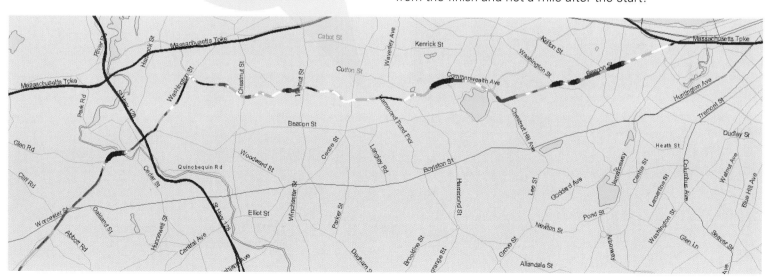

April 19 was hot—bad for runners—but with strong winds from the west, good conditions for the wheelchair event. Ernst Van Dyk of South Africa set a new world record for a wheelchair marathon, and Tim posted a new personal best of 1:51:13. Congratulations, Tim!

GPS and golf

Although I like to whack golf balls at a driving range, I don't seem to have the patience or discipline for all that other stuff you must do to succeed: putting, difficult approach shots, and so forth. So it never occurred to me to do a page on golf in the book.

On April 22, I had enough book material prepared to present it to GDT employees in our internal "Know-More-Café" lecture series. I discussed GPSing outdoor activities and showed some of the images and maps I had made for the book.

I came in to work the next Monday and found the following message from coworker Paul Dixon:

Dear Mr. Cooke,

Thanks for sparking my imagination with your presentation! I have been a GPS hobbyist for about 4 years and have primarily used my Garmin eMap® for in-car navigation and finding the nearest McDonalds® to get my daughter a Happy Meal® on road trips.

I am an avid golfer and after your presentation I decided to take my GPS to the golf course to collect the waypoints of the centers of the greens and also to track my round. The waypoints will come in handy the next time I play so that I can determine the exact distance to the center of the greens on my approach shots.

The track will show me what a round of golf would look like from space. I did some searching online and found this website that had some very good links to some of the programs you mentioned and some that you might have not heard of.
http://www.digitalgrove.net/Toolbox_GPS.htm
I used the USAPhotoMaps program to plot my track as well as the waypoints of the centers of the greens and have attached the resulting image.

Thanks again for sparking my imagination and good luck with the book.

Best regards,
Paul

What's the lesson here? Don't allow yourself to be limited by my lack of imagination and experience! Try different stuff with your GPS. You won't know if it works unless you try it. Thanks, Paul!

GPS on the water

Speaking of water . . . one of life's enduring questions:

Will my GPS float if I drop it in the water?

Garmin claims that its GPSMAP 76 model will float. Do you believe this? In the interest of science, I decided to run a test.

The good ship Garmin floats fine and even continues to compute latitude and longitude. But be warned, most other GPS models will sink. Don't conduct your experiments in water over your head!

"Can I GPS my scuba trip?"

Sorry, no.

Despite the fact that the Garmin 76 will float, and that most GPSs are designed to survive a submersion standard of thirty minutes under a meter of water, your GPS won't compute positions even a quarter-inch below water. The water acts as a shield that the GPS signals can't penetrate. Even just the liquid inside your hand will prevent the signals from reaching the GPS antenna; clasp your hand over the antenna of your operating GPS to verify this.

Still getting weak signals from three satellites (see bars), but bravely reporting a 3-D differential fix. Don't believe it; you can't get 3-D with three satellites. I bet Garmin's extrapolation algorithm is doing the talking.

GPSMAP has a ten-satellite fix, but must take a dip to answer the scuba question.

Note: The bucket contains fresh water. Salt water will get into the battery compartment and short out the batteries, stopping the GPS. If this happens, just rinse thoroughly in fresh water and dry before reinstalling batteries. A sturdy reclosable plastic bag is a good precaution in either salty or fresh water.

Barely submerged, but deaf to the world of satellites.

Mapping your windsurfer

As founder of GDT (now part of Tele Atlas), I often get to meet customers and business partners when they visit us in New Hampshire. While visiting GDT several years ago, Dr. Charles Ivey, president of Tobin International, spotted a picture of me windsurfing in Aruba with my kids. "I sail too; I just clocked over 30 mph on my board," he claimed.

I knew that the Texas gulf coast has good wind, so I asked Dr. Ivey if that was at a special windsurfer speed trench set up with timing instrumentation. No, he said, he just stuck his GPS in a resealable plastic bag and taped it to the mast.

What a fun thing to try; why didn't I think of doing that? Next weekend I started carrying a GPS and waterproof bags with the rest of my windsurfing gear. I quickly learned that most plastic bags will rupture if you crash hard enough, and that salt water

will get into the battery compartment and short out the batteries. The cure is simply a quick fresh-water rinse 'n' dry cycle; the delicate innards of GPS receivers seem well protected from water.

Now that I've accumulated a bunch of GPSs for this book, I tape two Garmin 76 units to the mast, just above the boom, so I have a speedometer visible for each tack.

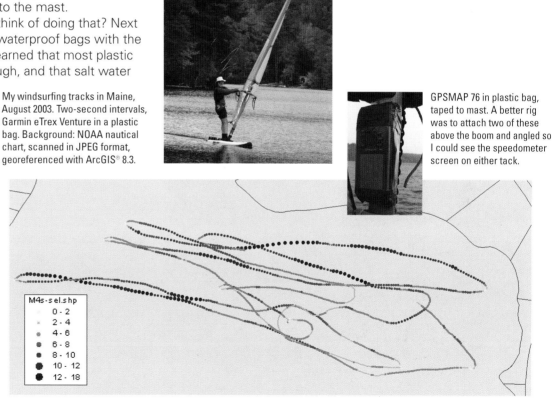

My windsurfing tracks in Maine, August 2003. Two-second intervals, Garmin eTrex Venture in a plastic bag. Background: NOAA nautical chart, scanned in JPEG format, georeferenced with ArcGIS® 8.3.

GPSMAP 76 in plastic bag, taped to mast. A better rig was to attach two of these above the boom and angled so I could see the speedometer screen on either tack.

M4s-sel.shp
- 0 - 2
- 2 - 4
- 4 - 6
- 6 - 8
- 8 - 10
- 10 - 12
- 12 - 18

Another of my windsurfing tracks, this time at Post Pond in Lyme, June 2004. South wind's good for this pond; contrast this with Dan O'Hara's tracks in a northwest wind a few months before (page 32).

Anna Lee and Annaliesse go to Antarctica

When Annaliesse Hyser was twelve years old, she made up her mind to visit every continent. By the time she graduated from Swarthmore, she had visited all but Antarctica through family or college travels. Her workmate Anna Lee jumped at the chance to accompany her on a cruise to her last continent.

Getting there is half the fun: a long flight to Buenos Aires, just in time to greet the new year in Argentina's early summer. Then down to Ushuaia to board the *Professor Multanovskiy,* a Russian research vessel converted to cruise ship.

Anna and Annaliesse gamely took one of my Geko GPS units, set up to record one point every ten seconds, and turned it on in various places during the trip. The points they captured definitely prove that GPS is a global system, working perfectly less than 1,800 miles from the South Pole.

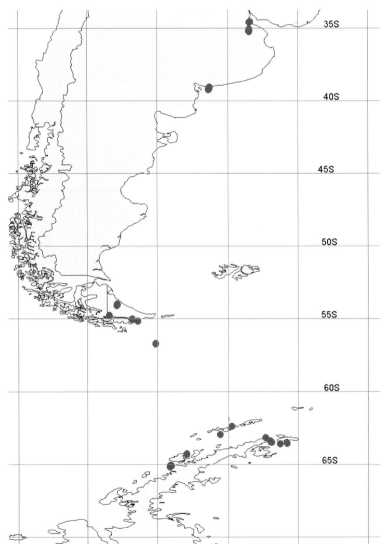

MN DNR - Garmin

File   Edit   GPS   Waypoint   Track   Route   Real Time   Help

Geko 201 Software Version 2.20

Lat   Lon
Alt   EPE   <<< Data Table <<<

○ Waypoint   ● Track   ○ Route   ○ RTimeWpt

	type	ident	lat	long	y_proj
287	TRACK	ACTIVE LOG	-65.10367155	-64.04020786	6268.08
288	TRACK	ACTIVE LOG	-65.10362864	-64.04016495	6263.60
289	TRACK	ACTIVE LOG	-65.10360718	-64.04018641	6261.09
290	TRACK	ACTIVE LOG	-65.10358572	-64.04022932	6258.44
291	TRACK	ACTIVE LOG	-65.10360718	-64.04037352	6259.87
292	TRACK	ACTIVE LOG	-65.10358572	-64.04052973	6256.55
293	TRACK	ACTIVE LOG	-65.10352135	-64.04065847	6248.61
294	TRACK	ACTIVE LOG	-65.10345697	-64.04072285	6241.08
295	TRACK	ACTIVE LOG	-65.10341406	-64.04076576	6236.06
296	TRACK	ACTIVE LOG	-65.10334969	-64.04074430	6229.07
297	TRACK	ACTIVE LOG	-65.10324240	-64.04067993	6217.60
298	TRACK	ACTIVE LOG	-65.10302792	-64.04042244	6195.45

Connected   0 of 666 Selected

Minus 65 degrees latitude. *"Toto, I don't think we're in Kansas anymore."*

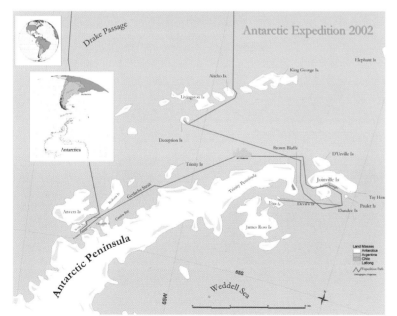

Chris Mabey runs GDT's Mapping Services Department. He took a similar cruise two years ago. His cartographic record of the trip is a tribute to the skills of real mapmakers.

Anna and Annaliesse's Geko unit shows that they visited most of the same spots that Chris did on his cruise.

Dartmouth sailing team

Dartmouth always has a strong sailing team, and Coach Brian Doyle invited me out to Lake Mascoma to GPS an afternoon practice. My daughter Abby had raced for Yale, and was home from Thailand for her sister's college graduation. Abby helped attach and retrieve Garmin GPSMAP 76 units, run the launch Brian provided us, and explain the intricacies of dinghy racing to me as I took pictures. The usual one-point-per-second setting provided useful and appealing track logs.

Abby retrieves a GPS.

Amory Loring and Scott Hogan were both named to the 2004 ICSA All-America sailing team.

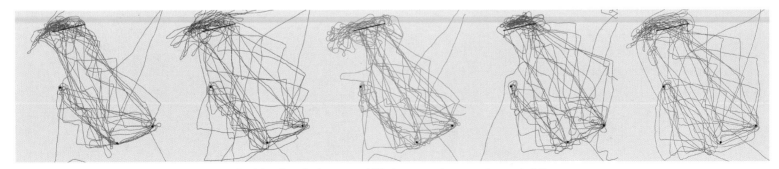

Track logs from five boats reveal differing approaches to an afternoon's drill.
Twelve boats in the water; only six GPSs. Still plenty of data to map.

Boat number 3 won the heat mapped below by choosing the simplest course (red dots). The second boat to finish, number 20, sailed at a higher average speed and covered more distance (blue dots).

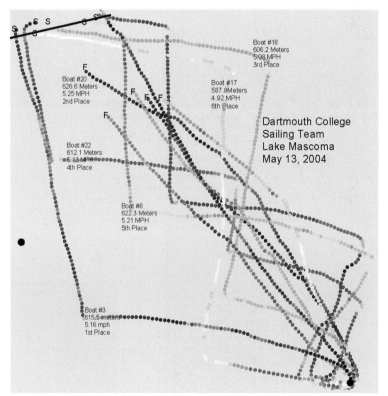

Boat #18
606.2 Meters
5.08 MPH
3rd Place

Boat #20
626.6 Meters
5.25 MPH
2nd Place

Boat #17
587.8 Meters
4.92 MPH
6th Place

Dartmouth College
Sailing Team
Lake Mascoma
May 13, 2004

Boat #22
612.1 Meters
5.13 MPH
4th Place

Boat #8
622.3 Meters
5.21 MPH
5th Place

Boat #3
615.5 meters
5.16 mph
1st Place

Kenduskeag Stream Race

Here's how to shake off winter blahs and get through Mud Season: enter your canoe or kayak in the annual Kenduskeag Stream Race. This year, 1,024 paddlers in 570 boats took part in the 16-mile run from Kenduskeag, Maine, to Bangor.

By 7:30 A.M. on race day I had a Geko taped to a thwart on Shawn Kennedy and Don Hummels' number 59 canoe. To answer their "why did you pick us?" question, I just pointed to the row of decals from previous events and evidence of meticulous preparation, right down to the row of candy bars strategically taped along the gunwales.

Next, the number 1 on the bow of a 26-foot-long war canoe caught my eye. First to finish last year, J.R. Mabee, Leslie Mabee, Tammy Kelley, Ander Thibaud, Bill Smith, and John Cangelosi were shooting to break a war-canoe class record that had stood for eleven years. Captain Mabee decided that a 3-ounce Geko wouldn't slow them much, so Tammy's water cooler doubled as a GPS mount.

I stopped twice along the stream to take pictures. When I got to the finish, the number-1 boat was long gone. I congratulated Shawn and Don when number 59 finished and retrieved their GPS. I found one of the war-canoe team members and got directions to J.R.'s house to get the other Geko. Back home, number 59's track looked "nominal":

Canoe #59

War canoe #1

But what about number 1's Geko? What were these other lines? Answer: my Geko had run the stream; they'd loaded the canoe on a van, driven back up to Kenduskeag to pick up another vehicle, then returned home, with the little GPS still faithfully logging both the canoe and vehicle tracks.

Most spectators camp out at Six Mile Falls, an optional portage that's tricky enough to merit dry-suited rescue teams in the water to help less-skilled boaters. J.R. had told me they would portage, as the long canoe was difficult to maneuver, and a well-executed portage was faster than running.

The ever-popular (and fast) Gumby canoe runs Six Mile Falls.

Six Mile Falls: Run or portage?

GPS time stamps settle the question: number 59's well-executed rapids run took 4 minutes and 48 seconds (between the orange marks in the map above). The war canoe's portage took only 3 minutes, 26 seconds. And yes, they did clip over six minutes off the old course record!

Warm-up for the Worcester Regatta

Several years ago, Hanover High School became the first public high school in New Hampshire to have a varsity girls' crew. Community fund-raising financed five eight-person shells, oars, and outboard launches for the coaches. I showed up for a foggy 5:30 A.M. practice, along with fifty-four students. And I thought only hockey players turned out for early-morning practices!

I duct-taped Garmin GPSMAP 76 units just behind the steering mechanism and set the track logs to record one point per second. I rode along in Coach Julie Stevenson's launch to take pictures.

If I were to try this again, I would either use an external antenna or figure a way to mount the GPSMAP 76 upright. This model's internal antenna works best upright, and the second varsity boat's GPS didn't lock onto a fix until a mile upstream. But both devices were working fine when Coach Stevenson ran a simulation of the 500-meter race coming up at the Worcester Regatta. GPS analysis shows the first boat consistently maintaining more than 9 mph throughout the course, enough to beat the second boat to the finish by five seconds.

Vermont .5-meter orthophoto taken in 1994 captured two crew shells on the river.

Color coding by speed reveals rhythm of dawn practice session; darkest colors indicate speeds over 11 mph.

Hanover High School
Prep for Worcester Regatta
500 meter course
May 20, 2004, 6:15 AM

Time-slice.shp
1st-race.shp
- 0.65 - 9
- 9 - 9.5
- 9.5 - 10
- 10 - 10.5
- 10.5 - 11
- 11 - 11.5
- 11.5 - 12

2nd-race.shp
- 0.32 - 9
- 9 - 9.5
- 9.5 - 10
- 10 - 10.5
- 10.5 - 11
- 11 - 11.5
- 11.68

First Varsity: Red: 1:51
Second Varsity: Blue: 1:56

Green at 10-second intervals

Shelling on North Captiva

In January, our friends Beman and Sonda Dawes invited my wife Jennifer and me to share their rental apartment on Sanibel Island. Not only did we all get our first geocaching experience (page 4), but we GPSed the shelling trip we took to North Captiva Island.

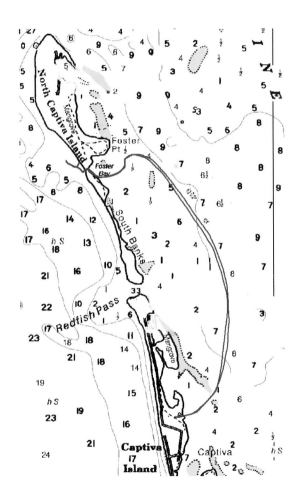

Captain John Salus didn't need any of my GPS gear; he had his own Garmin marine unit mounted on the control panel.

Beman shows Gilsson external antenna taped inside cap. Sharp-eyed computer nerds will spot Beman's C++ T-shirt; he's a member of the C++ standards committee and the founder of *boost.org*.

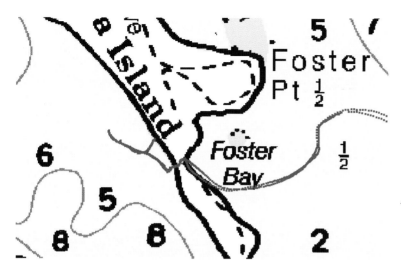

So what's going on here? We landed in Foster Bay and walked about 100 yards to the west shore for shelling and bird watching. We didn't go in the water, and the GPS was receiving as many satellites as I've ever seen. Why does our track plot out in the water? I know shorelines can change overnight in storms*, and the NOAA data sets I had downloaded were old versions. I bought a current paper chart, expecting to see a major shoreline change. No significant difference. I don't know what's going on. I believe the GPS. If you're in the neighborhood, walk the west shoreline in this area and get an accurate track log. Perhaps I'll go back and do this someday.

* Yes! On August 13, 2004, Hurricane Charlie cut North Captiva Island in half!

Jenny demonstrates an experienced sheller's "Sanibel Stoop."

Few visitors to North Captiva means relatively tame sea birds.

Airborne GPS

GPS is standard equipment in most aircraft these days. In fact, the Wide Area Augmentation System (WAAS), which doubles the accuracy of our GPSs, is a Federal Aeronautics Administration (FAA) initiative.

Airborne applications are particularly fun and challenging because they bring issues of elevation—the third dimension—into play.

Normal 2-D GIS mapping of a skydiver's track, for example (pages 86–87), conceals lots of action; here's Slick and Derek's wingsuit jump as seen from above:

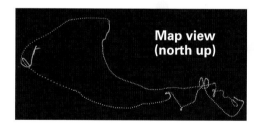

Map view (north up)

Derek (green) leaves the jump plane a couple of seconds before Slick (blue), at the left side of the view. They diverge almost immediately, with Derek heading northeast and Slick turning southeast. Then both head east and maneuver for landing.

Viewed from the side with the ESRI ArcView® 3D Analyst™ extension, you get a different picture. Slick and Derek actually did more than 7,000 feet of free-fall and wingsuit flight in close proximity before diverging to deploy canopies. Canopy deployment slows vertical and horizontal speed; the one-per-second dots get much closer together.

This is just one 3-D view; on the computer screen you can rotate the viewpoint for analysis.

Side view from south

The 3D Analyst extension is designed and priced for professional use, but there are other inexpensive special-purpose packages that are fun for 3-D display.

Can you decouple your vision and see 3-D with two images? Try this with the end of Slick and Derek's ride, below, as seen from the east:

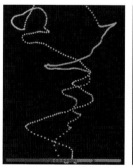 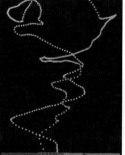

Make stereo pairs by grabbing two screen shots, rotating the image slightly between them.

GPSing a model airplane

Since 1986, Peter Moeykens has been the principal designer and author of GDT's production mapping software. In this capacity he has written about a million lines of computer code, in FORTRAN, DataPower, and now C++.

So how does Pete find time to build model airplanes? We're not just talking control-line models either, but a radio-controlled helicopter and a scale DC-3 with operating hydraulic landing gear.

When I asked Pete if he had any aircraft that could haul an 8-ounce Garmin GPSMAP 76, he recalled a plane he had built years ago to carry video cameras and transmitters. It was up in the attic and a bit dusty, but Pete assured me he could get it flying again.

We called around to find a safe place to fly. Larry Kelly in Dartmouth College's real estate office okayed Fullington Farm, as long as I cleared it with Scott Stokoe, who runs Dartmouth's organic farm on the site. Scott said fine, so at the end of a workday, Pete and I headed out to try the GPS.

No wheels, so hand-launch

GPS weight was no problem, but size of the GPSMAP unit dictated an awkward orientation. We taped an external antenna inside the fuselage for best reception.

Thanks, Pete, Larry, and Scott!

Dead-stick landing harvested weeds but did no damage.

Check the GPS: yes, we got a track; we're done!

GPSing a model airplane (continued)

As I usually do with GPS tracks, I opened the text (.txt) file I saved from DNR Garmin in Microsoft Excel and ran speed calculations (see page 125). I then deleted superfluous track points (for example, showing Pete and I walking from his truck to the field). I also looked for sudden speed changes; these usually are spurious, due to a GPS error for a second or two. Often I can move a couple of bad points and recalculate speeds to clean up the data.

I did this with the "zinger" shown in the orthophoto map at the lower right. Then I saw the zigzag tracks (green lines in the enlarged portion of the map, at right) and couldn't make sense of them. I enlarged this section for Pete and displayed altitude at each point. Pete reminded me that he had flown two loops in succession, each taking about four seconds. With the GPS logging one point per second, I only had eight data points to represent both loops. As with Bucky Demers' car 26, Pete's airplane is just too fast for the GPS to record details of its track!

Raw data looks good at a glance; closer inspection reveals GPS anomalies. Pete was having too much fun to keep the up-side up and the down-side down. I suspect the Garmin lost satellite lock when the plane was inverted in loops, unleashing some loss-of-signal gremlins.

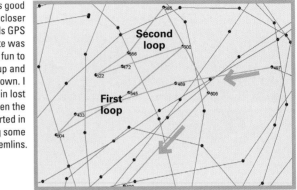

Jeff Bogan's 3-D Tracer program shows 3-D tracks and lets you relive your flight in animation; see *www.stransim.com*. You'll also need G7TOWIN to download GPS tracks in .igc format. Do a Web search to find this.

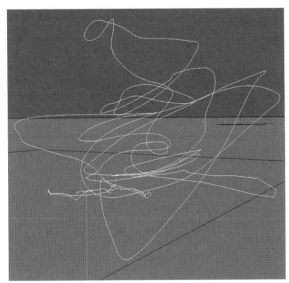

Zinger ("spear") resulting from single erroneous coordinate

Boland balloon

Brian Boland built his first balloon in 1970 as an art project at Pratt Institute. A year later he flew his art project, and has been hooked on ballooning ever since. He bought the Post Mills airport in 1989 and built an ingenious structure housing perhaps the funkiest museum in New England, along with a huge sunny loft for cutting and sewing balloons.

Our house in Lyme is situated such that following a cold-front passage, the waning evening winds often bring Brian overhead. Many times our fields have provided the landing site at the end of a charter ride or the test flight of a new balloon. More than once Brian has invited members of my family to accompany him, right from our backyard, on the last leg of a flight.

Brian reinforces balloon edges subject to fraying. He's built 133 balloons and six airships (blimps) in the past thirty-three years. His ability to optimize balloons for various competitive classes has helped him set dozens of world records for distance, duration, and altitude. He's also towed a water skier behind a balloon on nearby Lake Fairlee, used a rowboat as a balloon basket for airborne fishing, and even converted a Volkswagen® chassis to serve as a self-retrieving balloon basket.

Surprisingly, there aren't many great places to attach GPSs on some balloons. Here I'm using duct tape to hold a Garmin GPSMAP 76 on the propane line. I really didn't want to get any of my units too near that burner!

Boland balloon (continued)

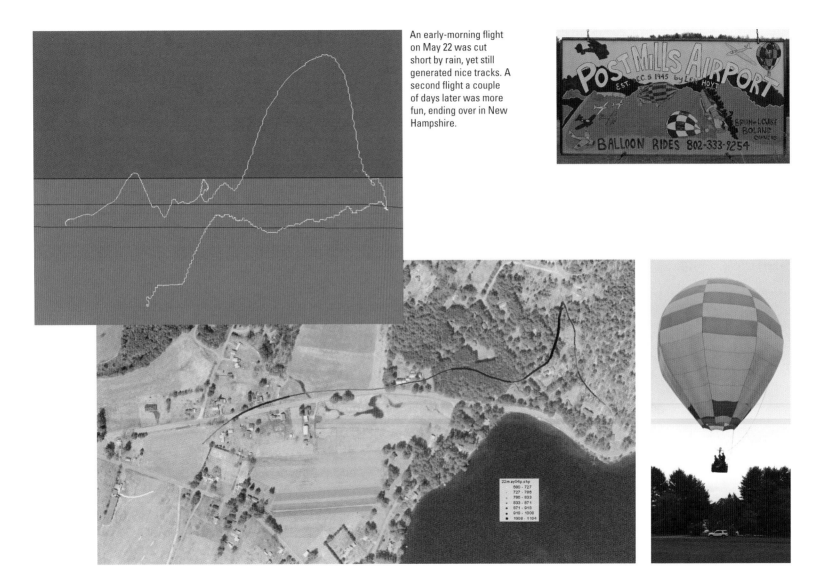

An early-morning flight on May 22 was cut short by rain, yet still generated nice tracks. A second flight a couple of days later was more fun, ending over in New Hampshire.

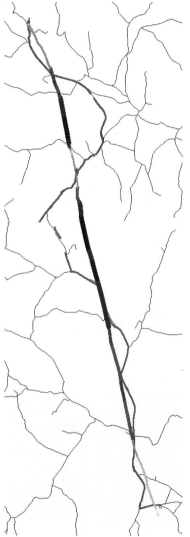

Brian's balloon *Independence* heads straight north-northwest in a strong steady wind. Darker red means higher altitude. A GPS left running in the chase car shows winding route home over the roads (blue).

Another flight a week later featured winds near maximum for launch with paying passengers. Jeff and Jane help Brian inflate *Independence*.

Hop in, let's go; it'll be a lot more stable up in the air.

Jeff and Jane used pictures from this flight in their wedding announcement.

Post Mills Soaring Club

Brian Boland's airport is also a haven for sailplane and taildragger enthusiasts. Of my friends in the club, Rick Sheppe was flying the L19 towplane on May 1; he encouraged me to GPS all the club aircraft. Duct tape and a mix of Gekos and GPSMAPs with external antennas allowed me to capture some beautiful flight paths. All units were set to record one track point per second.

Rick turns final to land and tow the next sailplane.
Yellow tape holds Geko to L19's cockpit strut.

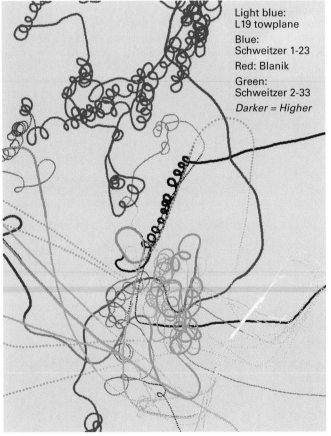

Light blue:
L19 towplane

Blue:
Schweitzer 1-23

Red: Blanik

Green:
Schweitzer 2-33

Darker = Higher

If you know about soaring, you'll spot the southwest takeoff and recognize the standard separation maneuvers that have the sailplanes (blue, red, green) releasing the towrope and immediately turning right, with the towplane (light blue) turning left to return to the field. Everyone can see the classic corkscrew turns to stay in thermals, which are being blown toward the northeast.

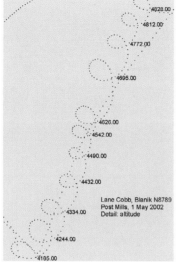

4828.00
4812.00
4772.00
4695.00
4626.00
4542.00
4490.00
4432.00
4334.00
4244.00
4185.00

Lane Cobb, Blanik N8789
Post Mills, 1 May 2002
Detail: altitude

Lane gets ready to solo the Blanik. Geko taped behind shoulder records thermaling.

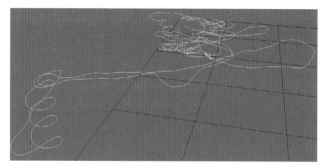

Jeff Bogan's 3-D Tracer program was designed
for sailplane pilots; see page 80.

Steve Voigt, who runs King Arthur Flour, first soloed last year. He had the best
ride of the day, staying aloft 1 hour and 35 minutes after a four-minute tow.

Skydiving

I got skunked twice by rain and high winds trying to GPS sky-divers, and then this turned out to be the most technically challenging project in the whole book. Not everything worked. A Foretrex on your wrist doesn't seem to see enough open sky in free fall. Helmet-mounted Gekos did better. The biggest challenge is to keep the GPS "hot" in the plane just before you step out into the slipstream.

In 1959 the first purpose-built sport parachuting center in the United States opened in Orange, Massachusetts. Just two hours down the road from my home, this was clearly the place to go. Not knowing much about sport parachuting, I was concerned that attaching a GPS to a helmet might be a safety hazard. Staff videographer Jeff Agard quickly dispelled my worries: his problem was finding vacant real estate for a Geko on his headgear:

Jumptown's Otter hauls twenty jumpers almost 3 miles up in eighteen minutes. Stan Snigir always beat everyone back down to earth by a large margin. There's a good reason for this; he's the U.S. speed skydiving champion. Stan tried a Foretrex on one jump and pocketed a Geko for another.

The sport has moved way beyond jumping out and pulling the D-ring. Nikolai Mosesov's wingsuit caught my eye; he tried one of my Foretrexes.

Wingsuits have sophisticated baffled airfoils that yield glide ratios around 3:1. You fly 3 miles overland for each mile you drop.

Brian "Slick" Lutton and Derek Landry also fly wingsuits. Here's their jump from 14,000 feet on June 27. Horizontal speed is what you want; it's displayed in color. I misinterpreted the tracks on the first go-round, but much e-mailing with Jeff and Brian set me straight. Brian (like most serious skydivers) wears a recording barometric altimeter that provided key data. Also—*duh*—my GPSs record elevation above sea level. The jumpers all think in terms of height above ground. And we had winds aloft ranging from 25 to 40 mph from the west. I'm not sure how you factor that into the analysis.

The other holy grail for skyfliers is glide ratio. I mapped this ratio for Brian's flight and selected 40 seconds during which he traveled 3,430 feet horizontally while only dropping 625 feet (the yellow track in the map below). This yields a 5.5:1 ratio, though I later found that Brian's canopy was already deployed. But there's a lot of potential for fun with GPS in this sport!

Office of Geographic and Environmental Information (MassGIS),
Commonwealth of Massachusetts Executive Office of Environmental Affairs

Office of Geographic and Environmental Information (MassGIS),
Commonwealth of Massachusetts Executive Office of Environmental Affairs

Brian bought himself a Geko 301
after seeing these maps.

Cool and comfortable: Derek
wears sandals when he jumps.

Morningside Flight Park

I tried a Rogallo hang glider in the 1970s, and it seemed a natural for GPSing. I had no idea that I was living just 40 miles from Morningside Flight Park, a mecca for the sport.

Best of all, I met Paul Moncure, a hang glider instructor, at a GDT new-employee briefing session. Paul invited me down to Morningside to see how the sport has advanced in thirty years.

Though Morningside lies on the Vermont–New Hampshire border, people have flown to both the Connecticut and New Hampshire coasts from the top of the hill. With overcast skies and no thermals, there weren't going to be any records broken the day I was there, just a crisp demonstration of the state of the art by Paul.

I taped a Garmin GPSMAP to Paul's variometer (vertical airspeed meter) and set it to store one point per second.

Keith Jacoby, up from New Haven, lent "Lavender Lady" to Paul for the GPS test and provided a lift to the summit launch site. Paul's flying suit incorporates an emergency parachute, serves as streamlining, and is insulated for warmth at high altitudes.

High-tech window seat

Back in chapter 1, I described how you can use a GPS with paper maps to help identify sights out the window. By now you know you can also collect and map track logs of your travels. I do this every time I'm flying and have a window seat.

GPS works on time signals; each of your track points is tagged with a super-accurate time stamp. Your digital camera probably also has an internal clock that time-stamps each picture. If I see something interesting out the window, I'll take some pictures knowing that I can match the time stamps on the pictures with one of my track points and have a good idea of where I took the picture.

If you want to do this, make sure you set the clock in your camera! If you're really picky, you can take a picture of the GPS screen that displays the time.

Here's a close-up from a picture I took of a GPS screen on May 13, 2004, at 9:19:55 P.M.:

How can we find out the time the camera's clock showed? Answer: open the image file with Microsoft Notepad! You'll see something like this:

At the beginning of most image files there's an EXIF header. EXIF stands for Exchangeable Image File Format; it contains lots of "metadata," or information about the image information that follows. Most of this info is gobbledygook, but you'll see date and time from the camera clock in several places. (Warning: if you rotate or otherwise modify your pictures, the EXIF data will be spoiled.)

When my camera took the picture, its clock read 21:18:42, or 9:18:42 P.M. I subtract this from the GPS time shown in the picture, and find that the camera clock is running one minute and thirteen seconds slow. Camera clocks are pretty stable, so my time difference will be good for all pictures I took that day.

To match the GPS track log with pictures, I'll have to add 1:13 to the camera time before selecting the corresponding track point. I'll also have to remember that the track log time stamps are in Universal (Greenwich mean) time.

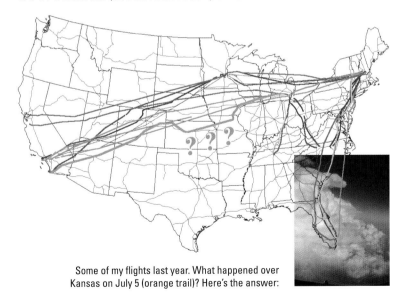

Some of my flights last year. What happened over Kansas on July 5 (orange trail)? Here's the answer:

Your GPS can tell you where you are in flight. Can it also tell your computer, so it can plot where you are in real time? No problem—other than your laptop's battery capacity and that guy who keeps reclining the seat in front of you.

Here's what this can look like. I'm running ESRI ArcMap™ 8.3 on my laptop with a Garmin 76 attached to the serial port. An external antenna is held between the window and shade using a pack of tissues as padding. ArcMap 8.3 has a GPS extension to get coordinates from the GPS. This lets me store my bread-crumb trail, display my track on the map, or even automatically pan when the track moves off the map display.

I captured a screen (below left) as we flew across southern Wisconsin last December; Lake Petenwell is off the left side of the plane. ArcMap 8.3 shows the GPS track along the bottom of the screen. Real-time GPS info is in the box at the top of the screen. The laptop display is remarkably similar to the scene out the window (below), except I can label towns, airports, and roads on the screen. If I honed my GIS skills I could have generated a perspective display, I suppose. I was happy just to get everything working at once!

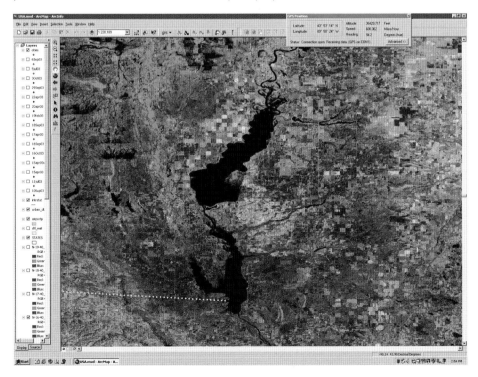

So what's that background image on my screen? Probably the best bargain in satellite data coverage: United States of America Digital Landsat Mosaics, brought to you by NASA and the USGS. Complete coverage of all fifty states, false color, 30-meter pixels, on four CDs. Sure, the images are pushing fifteen years old. I don't care! It's a wonderful resource for educators, GPSers, and window-seat fans.

Search the catalog at *core.nasa.gov.* I paid $25 for my CDs. If you're a teacher you might get them for less.

Oops . . .

Things happen. Every now and then when you're flying in a small airplane with the window open to take pictures, items tend to fall out, such as a running Garmin 76 GPS. If you're careful, you will have prepared for these contingencies by wrapping such objects in lots of bubble wrap so they won't be damaged or inflict damage upon contact with terra firma.

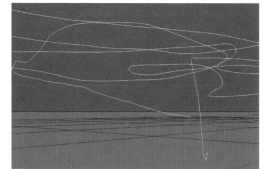

Jeff Bogan's 3-D Tracer program shows the GPS unit's trajectory. What looks like a bounce is just GPS "jitter" on the ground.

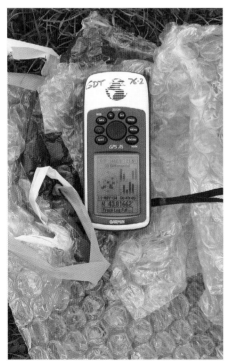

In this case, I managed to find the GPS in the woods after a few minutes of searching. The sturdy GPS was running fine, though the track log was full. I downloaded the track log for mapping and analysis.

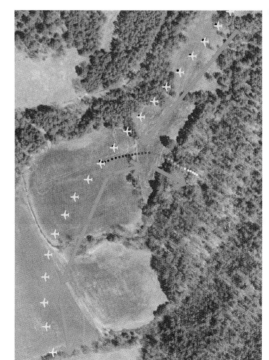

Why no graceful parabola? The bubble-wrapped GPS unit weighed less than a pound and had a lot of wind resistance. The plane and unit were flying at 84 mph. GPS readings show the unit immediately stabilizing at its terminal velocity of 41 feet per second (28 mph). A west wind had 31 seconds to blow it 505 feet to the east during a 1,280-foot drop.

GPS in schools and the community

Chapter 8 already! I hope you've enjoyed the book so far and have learned some of the neat capabilities of GPS and GIS.

For myself and others here at Tele Atlas, this is just where the fun begins. While it's interesting to attach a GPS to something and map where that something goes, the fun is multiplied when you teach students about GPS and help them use this technology in the classroom or at a science fair.

We've run GPS exercises in all grades, from elementary to college, simply modulating the complexity of the exercises and the depth of science and math we present.

What I love about the GPS/GIS combination is that it fits into just about any curriculum. Science, geography, social studies, and math are logical places for GPS and GIS, but so is history: navigation and mapmaking were major driving forces in the development of the scientific method. Several times when I've reviewed latitude and longitude with middle schoolers, they've just covered the British Empire in the nineteenth century and can see the political background for the 1884 treaty establishing Greenwich as the origin of longitude.

GPS and GIS are technologies that are being rapidly assimilated into our lives just as word processing and spreadsheets were in the 1980s. Rather than try to fit GPS and GIS into the curriculum, just present them as technologies to be learned along with word processing, spreadsheets, Web searching, digital photography, or video editing. There'll be plenty of opportunities to use these technologies in class projects and science fairs.

Beyond educational applications of GPS and GIS, there are also many community applications. Trail mapping for recreation, invasive species mapping for environmental monitoring, mapping to support therapeutic exercise, and establishing and monitoring conservation easements are representative examples.

Consumer GPS is a wonderful spin-off of U.S. military technology—perhaps second only to the Internet—and it's very rewarding to assist in applying it to civilian uses.

Originally, I had planned to include a chapter on schools and another on GPS in the community. As I researched local examples, I realized that this was an artificial distinction, as you'll see in a few pages.

GDT—now Tele Atlas—has been pushing GPS/GIS technology into schools and communities for years; we've won national recognition doing this. I'll describe a few GPS exercises we take on the road and use when school classes come visiting. I'll also introduce you to some people who are using this technology to make a difference in their schools and communities.

GPS Treasure Hunt

The GPS Treasure Hunt has been a staple of GDT and Tele Atlas' educational outreach. It's a really simple exercise, rich with learning potential:

1 Beforehand, hide the treasure and determine an accurate lat/long reading. Carefully copy these coordinates for each participant.

2 In class, quickly review the basics of latitude and longitude.

3 Move outside, hand out GPS receivers, and deliver the short version of how to run them.

4 Give the students the treasure coordinates and turn them loose!

At GDT and Tele Atlas, we've used treasure hunts with classes ranging from fifth grade through college. A warning, however: participants must be able to make sense of spatial abstractions; you may only bewilder children younger than middle-school age.

Lindsay homes in on the goal.

Andy tried the Go To function, but messed up entering one coordinate digit. Lesson: coordinates are great for computers but perilously fragile for humans.

Inexpensive inflated globe is a must for lat/long review.

You're probably thinking this is just a custom geocaching exercise: input the treasure coordinates as a waypoint and turn on the Go To function. Right? You could do this, I suppose, but you would miss a great educational opportunity.

Here's a better learning experience: most students don't know about waypoints, so we ask them just to look at the coordinates on the GPS display and the slip of paper with the treasure coordinates, then think about where they have to move to make these numbers match. Try doing this; it's not easy. Finding the treasure tests your understanding of how coordinates work outdoors in the real world, and makes you confront simple questions: "Which way is north, anyway?"

Succeeding in the hunt requires that one formulate a strategy and act on it. Usually kids try to match one coordinate, then the second one. If they need an extra challenge, start them out so that they'll have to work their way around a building to get to the goal.

It helps to have several people assisting with the hunt, reminding kids to look out for cars, or intercepting the team that's resolutely and confidently heading in precisely the wrong direction and pulling it aside for a strategy review.

On one GDT visit I heard a teacher say, "We covered this in class, but it's different out in the world." The students usually notice this too.

Matt assures Andy that the treasure (a GDT pen) is a truly valuable reward for his efforts.

Thanks, Anne Mazur, for helping on a hot day!

Getting close: treasure is in the trunk of the tan Camry.

Jeff tells Cindy he's matched the coordinates. He's only 10 feet from the treasure; not bad for a $200 GPS.

Mapping Hurricane Hill

Five years ago, Michael Quinn and Cynthia (Cindy) Faughnan were in the first class of the Community Mapping Program held by the Vermont Institute of Natural Science (VINS) in partnership with the Orton Family Foundation. I already knew Cindy as a hockey mom; our daughters played on the team for which she was parent coordinator and I was assistant coach. Both teach at Hartford (Vermont) Memorial Middle School.

What was a middle-school English teacher doing in a GIS class? Michael and Cindy were part of a team known for getting their students out into the community for field trips and community projects. Community mapping seemed like an excellent fit and the team came out of the summer program ready to install ArcView software on the school's network and test their new skills on the next field trip. Unfortunately, the school administration restructured the teams so the mappers were on different schedules, and declared that community mapping was not to take place during class time.

Instinct and experience convinced the former team not to give up on what they thought was an excellent opportunity for place-based experiential learning. Michael presented a letter to the administration and board declaring that the mapping would proceed as an elective after school, on weekends, and during vacation.

And so it did. The team bought a Garmin 12 GPS and borrowed GIS-grade Trimble® GPSs from VINS. A ragtag army of kids learned the technology and tackled mapping the Hurricane Hill town forest. I loved seeing students running ArcView in the English classroom after school hours.

No student graduates from etymologist Michael Quinn's science class without GIS and GPS experience.

A major breakthrough for the team was formation of the Wellborn Ecology Fund within the Upper Valley Community Foundation. Michael and Cindy were among the first grant recipients; they got funding for twenty-five Garmin 76 GPS units. Now every student could learn and use this technology just as they could use word processing to write their reports.

Working with town conservation and recreation committees, the class laid a grid of 100-by-100-meter cells over the forest and sent teams of four students out with GPS receivers, cameras, and notebooks to inventory and map a grid cell.

After a few field trips, each team "owns" its grid cell. The students have inventoried each cell, photographed points of interest, described topography and their experiences in prose and poetry, and mapped the forest with a topographical rigor unattainable by all but professional surveyors before the GPS/WAAS era.

Run the numbers: each grid cell is a bit more than two acres. The town forest has 565 acres. When these students come back from college, their younger counterparts will still be contributing to the town's knowledge of this asset.

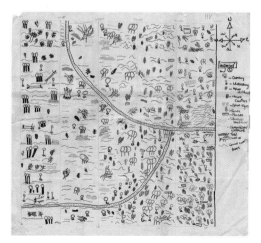

GPS units for each team ensured that 100-by-100-meter grid cells could be sewn together at their edges.

Already students have developed an interpretive trail brochure for the Department of Parks and Recreation and Conservation Commission. The brochure opens part of the forest to the rest of the community. This is but one of the GPS/GIS projects students have done; they've also worked on mapping the White River Watershed and compiled "Maps for the Heart" to aid fitness through the Good Neighbor Health Clinic.

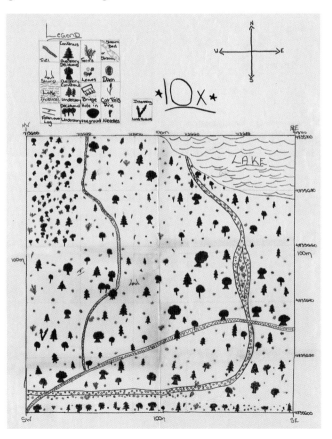

I love this kind of project. It covers the spectrum from technology to poetry. The kids learn without feeling they're being taught. They discover how to work in cross-functional teams, which is how a lot of things get done these days. They learn about their environment and community. They see class members they thought they had compartmentalized suddenly break out and take the lead in applying GPS or digital photography to a team effort. They get to present their work to the grown-ups. They're accepted as peers or even experts by the adults. They'll look back in a decade and recognize the contribution they made to their community.

Perhaps my favorite reaction to a school project was the head of a town conservation commission calling me after a sixth-grade GPS and mapping presentation asking if I could please teach the commission members whatever it was that those kids had learned!

What Michael and Cindy have accomplished hasn't been easy, but now their program is a going concern. They treat their stash of GPS devices as a community resource for other schools and organizations to borrow. They share their knowledge and experience with anyone who's interested. The work they and their students have done already benefits the community, and they've led their students on the important path of true citizenship.

Web sites   www.orton.org
www.communitymap.org
www.vinsweb.org/education/
community_map.html
www.hartfordsd.com/hmms/
Faughnan/orton/index.htm

English teacher Cynthia
Faughnan has taught me
useful undocumented
Garmin GPS features.

How does my GPS work?

I was one of those kids who built radios, made model airplanes, and took stuff apart to see how it worked. I still work on cars, mowers, and chain saws and occasionally perform autopsies on dead CD players. But fiddling with anonymous gray chips—instead of color-striped resistors and honking-big electrolytic capacitors you could charge up and then short out—isn't as much fun. Remember that elegant idea of having filament voltages add up to 117 volts so your radio didn't need a power transformer? Memory Lane isn't completely paved over quite yet.

There's still value in understanding how things work: cars, replay TVs, MRIs, touch-screen voting machines, camcorders, RFID, whatever. This applies to GPS also, and makes a nice exercise for middle schoolers. Often after running a GPS treasure hunt there's time to ask the students how they think their GPS knows where you are.

Does anyone know the answer?

"They work by satellites," someone responds.

Right, what do the satellites do?

"Your GPS asks the satellite to tell where you are and it returns the location."

Okay, except your GPS doesn't send out any signals. And none of the satellites know or care where you are.

"Um, well, the satellite . . . uh . . ."

Well, the satellites must be sending some signals that let each GPS figure out where it is, right?

"Right."

Can you figure out what these signals might say that would let the GPSs compute location?

"Um . . ."

Let's think about thunder and lightning. Does anyone know that thing you do with counting seconds from the lightning flash until you hear the thunder?

"Yes, yes, you count seconds: five seconds means the lightning struck a mile away."

OK, how does that work?

"Sound goes 1,000 feet per second so 5 seconds is 5,000 feet which is about a mile."

Good. Does everyone see how that works? The lightning gives us a signal that the sound message (thunder) is on the way, and the time it takes for the message to arrive tells us the distance to where the lightning struck. Now, if we saw the lightning hit a hilltop, we know that the hilltop has to be a mile away. If we don't know where we are, we can draw a circle with a radius of one mile around the hill. We have to be somewhere on that circle! If we were anywhere else, the thunder would have arrived earlier or later than 5 seconds.

Next, suppose we see lightning strike a tall building and we count 10 seconds before the thunder arrives. We're 2 miles from the building, right? What does that tell us about where we are? Another circle, centered on the building, with a 2-mile radius? And that circle has to touch the other circle, doesn't it? Probably in two places? (Draw pictures showing how circles can touch and intersect.)

Do you see how a third lightning strike would resolve which intersection we're at? Do you see how the idea of three messages—actually the length of time it takes three messages to arrive—can tell you where you are?

Well, we can't use thunder for GPS. Instead, each satellite has a clock and the message says what time it was when the message started. When my GPS receives the message, it records when the message arrived. The difference between that time and the time in the message tells the GPS how long it took for the message to get there. The GPS knows how fast the message travels: about 186,000 miles per second. So it can figure how far away the satellite was when it sent the signal.

Now, remember the black bars on the GPS screen? They show that the GPS has the "ephemeris" for that satellite. The ephemeris tells the GPS how to calculate where the satellite is at any point in time.

The GPS does this for at least four satellites. Each satellite's information locates the GPS somewhere on a sphere centered on the satellite. The GPS's computer calculates where the spheres intersect and converts that to latitude and longitude.

This is pretty much how GPS works. There are a couple more complications, but if you understand this much, you know more about how GPS works than 99 percent of the people in the world!

What did we do before GPS?

Well, we had LORAN (LOng RAnge Navigation). We had Transit. Before that we had sextants and chronometers, calibrated by radio. Before radio, you made sure the chronometer was wound regularly and hoped you understood whether it ran fast or slow. Before chronometers lots of ships ran up on the rocks; we had to depend on dead-reckoning and almost guess at longitude. Why is latitude easy to measure but longitude much harder? What's the logic for starting latitude at the equator? What's the reason the longitude starts at Greenwich? Does a compass always point north? Why doesn't a compass point toward the North Pole? At a given location, will my compass always point in the same direction?

Navigation and mapmaking have been important drivers for science and technology since the start of civilization. Modern science began with astronomy, a close cousin of geography and mapping. There are wonderful stories in the history of science and they make sense to students: What did we know back then? How did we know it? What did we know for sure that simply wasn't true? Why do most five-hundred-year-old maps show Antarctica, after which it disappears from maps in the 1700s? When did we know that Antarctica was there, anyway? What had to happen to change what we knew? How did our knowledge or ignorance of place affect our lives and nations?

All students memorize that the earth moves around the sun. How many of them complain that it sure looks like the earth is holding still and the sun is going around it? Not enough of them, I'm afraid.

Oh dear, don't get me started on this subject! But in the meantime, get a good, user-friendly sextant (Davis Mark 25) and have your students find where they are with a noon-sight. Tell John Harrison's story. Tell about the dog and the "powder of sympathy."

Seriously, we're way outside the scope of *Fun with GPS*, but the questions of where we are and how we know it fit across the curriculum and can fill in lots of gaps between science, history, and social studies.

Why did King George III pay £20,000 for a clock?

Why is this dude burning out his eyes looking at the sun?

Courtesy of National Oceanic and Atmospheric Administration/Department of Commerce

Mapping an old cemetery

This is frustrating for GPS fans. GDT has done some great projects with students and cemeteries, usually working with Valley Quest (page 106). Kids love a series of outdoor exercises combining GPS, database, and digital photography technologies with town history and the chance to express their feelings about a somewhat spooky subject in their journals. My frustration with cemetery mapping is that the gravestones are generally too close together to map accurately, even with a GIS-grade GPS unit.

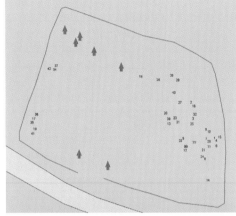

Even postprocessed Trimble GPS data required hand-tweaking to make this map. Gravestones are close together and the woodland setting is far from optimal for GPS accuracy.

Colleen Stevens is Tele Atlas' GPS expert: her geophysics PhD entailed months of survey-grade GPS recordings along earthquake faults in Indonesia.

At present, these images produced by fourth graders constitute the only record the town has of this part of its heritage. Small number signs link images to students' data sheets.

Magnetic vs. true north

This is a simple exercise. It's so quick that you can run it before or after a longer GPS project. Despite its simplicity, I strongly believe in the value of engaging students in real-world activities to reinforce a point. Here's how to do this:

We pick an arbitrary meridian of longitude: W 72.32100.

We unroll a second length of tape along a north–south line indicated by compasses. (Doing this part requires some negotiation and voting by class.)

The resulting angle graphically illustrates our magnetic declination: about 15.5 degrees west in the Connecticut River Valley.

We spread out along the line we create by moving back and forth to stay on the chosen meridian.

We unroll 125 feet of plastic tape to make our GPS meridian. The line points to true north.

All the material you'll need is a 1,000-foot roll of 3-inch plastic tape emblazoned with the message CAUTION BURIED UTILITY LINE BELOW. Costs about $20. Cut it into eight 125-foot sections. (I roll and store it on two reels intended for movable electric fencing.)

Check your declination results at *www.ngdc.noaa.gov/seg/geomag/jsp/Declination.jsp*.

Land conservation

Mike Smith and Lee Larson are from Planet Earth, despite the antennas on their hats. In fact, both are working to preserve portions of this planet through land trusts, conservation easements, and the Town Conservation Commission, of which Lee is the chairman. Both find GPS an essential tool in their work, supplementing their knowledge of land recordation and surveying practices.

They're both retired; Lee taught college physics; Mike ran a printing company. Mike was part of a neighborhood group that formed a town land trust in 1985; I worked with him for five years on the most complicated conservation project in the town's history. It didn't hurt that Mike was chairman of the century-old Society for Preservation of New Hampshire Forests at the time.

Part of any land project is going out on site and working with surveyors to ensure that boundaries are where they're meant to be and that abutting landowners agree with boundary definitions. Readers in Europe will be amazed to learn that the United States of the twenty-first century still follows eighteenth-century land recordation practices. In New England, the county simply registers deeds; it's up to buyers to search back into the early 1800s to see if the ownership chain is intact. Some towns have excellent parcel-level GIS coverage, down to building footprints. Others have just digitized their paper tax maps, perpetuating errors in a new medium. Really poor towns don't even have tax maps; this barrier to spatial knowledge will help keep them poor.

I joined Mike and Lee in researching boundaries of a parcel that Mike's daughter was planning to build on. They'd been out before and had found that somebody in 1909 had built a house

GPS won't replace paper maps but it sure helps relate
what's on the map with what's on the ground.

States vary all over the place on modernization of land records, as well as Internet access to parcel GIS data. North Carolina, Massachusetts, and Wisconsin are a few states that have pioneered recordation reform and access, recognizing that citizen access to uniform, timely, and accurate data is fundamental to a twenty-first-century economy. Maryland and Montana serve statewide parcel maps on the Web.

Want parcel data for your town? Try the portals on page 114. Hint: parcel data is often called the "cadastre" or "cadastral data," a term harking back to Napoleon's land reforms, which are part of the reason that most European countries have excellent land records. If the federal portals don't find your parcels, try the state GIS agency; see page 116 for how to locate it. As a last resort, I often call the town's tax assessor or GIS office if there is one. Sometimes the local regional planning commission can help. Good luck! Remember, your municipality isn't running on all cylinders if it doesn't have good, publicly available parcel GIS coverage.

nearby on land belonging to the town. I wanted to see how they were using GPS in their work.

I had uploaded digital parcel boundaries to my Garmin 76 unit's active track memory using the DNR Garmin program. In the field, we quickly discovered that several boundaries we were checking had been moved on the town maps, and I wasn't using the current copy. As a consequence, I was off by more than 100 feet in places.

In practice you end up attempting to reconcile four versions of the "truth" about a parcel boundary: what the tax map says, what the GPS shows, what the legal description says, and what's actually out there on the ground. The buyer must beware, or better yet, hire a lawyer to run a title search and a surveyor to flag the boundaries. Unfortunately, the good work done by these professionals is often just filed away; abutting property owners can't take advantage of accurate surveys of adjacent parcels.

Good parcel GIS coverage might prevent this kind of mistake. States with property taxes take pains to equalize tax burdens from town to town. What about ensuring that the property knowledge base is also accurate and equitable?

Enfield woman pays taxes on 6 acres for 40 years, had only 1 acre all along

And she can only get an abatement for one year's taxes

By Josh Adams
Staff Reporter

ENFIELD — Glenda Jarvis owes almost $2,500 this year in property taxes for her home and the surrounding land on Route 4. Since 1964 the town has collected for 6 acres according to the tax rates, but a recent survey showed she only owns the 1 acre on which her mobile sits.

Tracking museum visitors

Two years ago our regional science museum opened an out-door science park connected to miles of nature trails along the Connecticut River. What makes it popular? Which exhibits are "sticky," inducing people to linger at them, or come back two or three times during one visit? Could we use GPS to track museum visits? The accuracy should permit us to determine which exhibit is being visited, and time spent could be measured by the GPS time stamps.

Director David Goudy gave us the go-ahead to try GPS, and we decided to do it on the day of the Montshire Associates Spring Fling. I sent around a company e-mail to my GDT work-mates to see who was bringing their children to the event. I had my hands full with volunteers!

The first finding was that the GPS becomes an exhibit by itself. Several of the children never put it in a pocket or fanny-pack as we recommended. We can't claim that the GPS unob-trusively monitored these visits, but we were just testing the methodology.

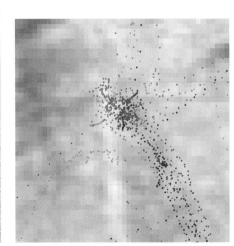

Nicholas observes shadows. This 2,200-pound granite globe's alignment shows the sun setting in Finland and about to rise in Japan. GPS tracks show every visitor passing by this exhibit at least once.

Science can be fun: Dominic (with my encouragement) measures the specific gravity of a Garmin 76.

Lots of hiking possibilities

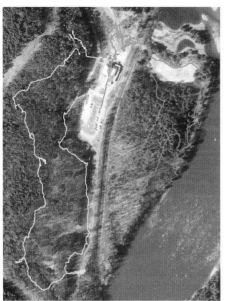

Billy and Jennifer Ulz (yellow) hiked trails west of the railroad tracks; Abigail and Samantha Downey (green) chose the riverside loop.

Samantha listens to water, below.

Billy and Jennifer test pebble sounds.

Repeat visits

12:12:45: 24 seconds   13:35:28: 32 seconds

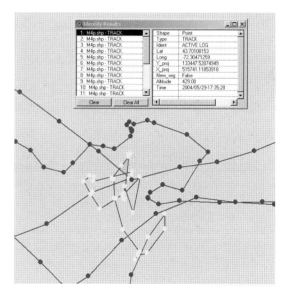

In addition to the two visits pictured above, the track log shows that Lucas and Anthony also walked past without stopping at 11:31:05 and again at 13:47:52.

Trail mapping

Julia Payne worked as an intern at Valley Quest* during her senior year at Dartmouth, and called GDT for assistance in mapping a trail for the Podunk Quest. We briefed her on running a Garmin GPSMAP 76 and promised the services of GDT cartographer Mike Griffin for the mapping.

There's more to making a good trail map than just collecting some track points; that's where Mike's training and experience come in. And Julia discovered—as we all do—that GPS reception along a wooded trail leaves a lot to be desired. I commend her resourcefulness in mounting the external antenna on a pole, and for collecting two sets of track points along with lots of waypoints along the trail.

As happens in the real world, Julia's two tracks failed to overlay in places. There are several ways to deal with this: one is to revisit the site and collect even more data. Instead, Mike and Julia consulted her notes, waypoints, and recollections, decided that the track discrepancies were legitimate GPS error, and defined the cartographic track by splitting the distance between the two GPS tracks.

www.vitalcommunities.org/ValleyQuest/resources.htm

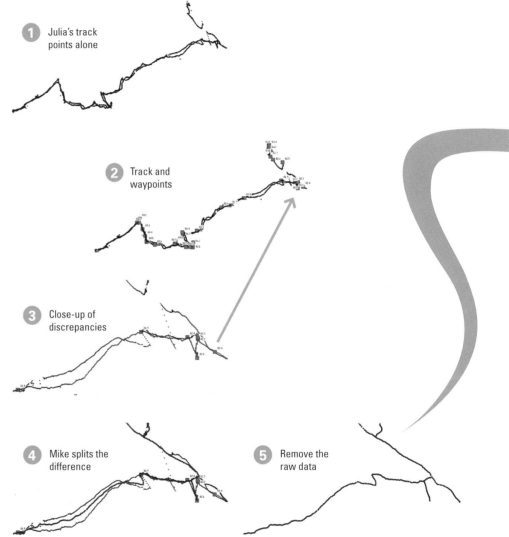

1. Julia's track points alone

2. Track and waypoints

3. Close-up of discrepancies

4. Mike splits the difference

5. Remove the raw data

Next, Mike brought in a digital orthophoto quad background and started thinking about how to make a black-and-white map communicate with the reader.

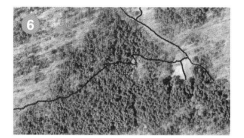

How can we see the trail line, especially when printed grayscale only?

Mike makes a copy of the trail line using a thicker, light-colored line.

The thicker, lighter copy behind the darker thin line makes the trail stand out. Now add waypoints.

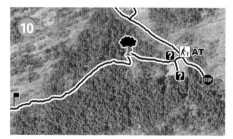

Almost done: change to monochrome and choose catchy symbols for points.

The final product

The Podunk Quest

Mike's final product just needs a symbol key. The map communicates what's needed to navigate, with no superfluous decoration to compete with the trail experience.

Making lat/long visible

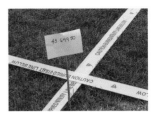

This is a wonderful picture. It's a detail from one of Robert Tinney's *Byte Magazine* covers from 1979; I have Collector Edition copy number 44 framed in my office. Check out *www.tinney.net* (alas, this print, "Perspectives," is sold out).

If you're a GPS true believer, you know this is what the world really looks like; why can't others see it this way? Here's a way to help them see the truth.

On a large athletic field, hand out WAAS-enabled GPS units set to display decimal latitude and longitude. (This is important; don't use minutes and seconds or projected coordinates.) Once everyone is showing black bars and "D"s, pick any starting latitude value ending with zero in the fifth decimal place. Have your GPS team spread out in a row about 100 feet long, with everyone moving back and forth perpendicular to the row to keep that zero in the last place. Remind students to hold their units high; we need maximum accuracy to make this work.

When the GPS line looks stable, unroll 125 feet of tape and pin it down with landscape staples.

As soon as the first line's in place, have everyone take a few steps and line up on the next zero. In the pictured example, we used latitudes 43.69940, 43.69950, 43.69960, and 43.69970. Do the same for four similar longitude values.

The grid takes form; are the boxes square? They don't look it. Measure each box to find out and get their average width and height. Uh-oh, they're not squares. Should they be squares? Did we mess up? Which distance is shorter, between latitudes or between longitudes? What's the ratio of the shorter dimension to the larger? (It's around .7 in New England.) What if we lived near

the North Pole and we tried this? How about near the equator? What would the ratios be in those places? Do the students know about functions, and specifically simple trig functions? What function would be 1 at the equator (latitude 0), around .7 where we are (latitude ~43), and 0 at the North Pole (latitude 90)?

Now roll up all 1,000 feet of tape and account for all of those wicked-sharp staples!

I love this exercise, but it is so busy and labor-intensive that we've only ever done it twice. Someday I'll make a time-lapse movie of the process.

Write your name with GPS

This is harder than it looks.

Can you visualize your name on an athletic field and then walk along the letters carrying a GPS, so that you write your name into the track log? Several times I've seen middle schoolers spontaneously try this as soon as they realize their GPS is plotting their track live as they move around. Cindy Faughnan assembled a group of her eighth graders to try this out.

We used Garmin 76 units, making sure we had WAAS enabled and all satellites working for us (black bars and little "D"s). We discussed how fast to move (slowly along letters; quickly between letters), and the merits of cursive versus block lettering.

I had tried this months before with my visualization aided by snow cover (footprints!). I thought I had a great idea: cover the GPS antenna while moving between letters! My message was "DON (heart) JENNY"!

Ooops, here's something to consider: Matt did a good job with his name, but wrote it from east to west while facing south. He inverts the GPS display to get the name upright on the GPS's map page but then the antenna faces down—not the best orientation for a good GPS fix.

Matt's saved track is highlighted on the display.

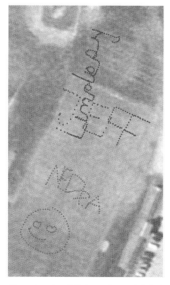

Huh? What happened? Covering the antenna didn't help at all! Tramping around in the snow, I evoked the Garmin extrapolation feature (see page 37) at least eight times. As the GPS restored lock after having the antenna covered, it resumed recording the track log as soon as it had a minimal position. The minimal position (four satellites for 3-D) is often 10, 20, or 30 feet or more from an accurate fix. See the "O" in "DON" for an example of this.

Some track points have been deleted to enhance readability.

Educational merit of this exercise? It probably doesn't fit into any standard curriculum. Does that disqualify it? It does reinforce mastery of a useful twenty-first-century technology.

Background data

One hundred and twenty years ago, John Wesley Powell, in an address to the U.S. Congress, declared that "A government cannot do any scientific work of more value to the people at large, than by causing the construction of proper topographic maps of the country." As the second director of the U.S. Geological Survey, Powell sold the nation on the utility of high-quality, publicly available, general-purpose maps depicting ubiquitous themes such as roads and rails, town and county boundaries, streams and ponds, elevation and settlements. Over a century later, Powell's vision was completed in the form of fifty-five thousand 7.5-minute quadrangle maps.

These maps belong to the citizens of the country and form the basis of development, conservation, planning, recreation, agriculture, transportation, and most importantly, further map-making. That's what this book is about, after all: the fun of making your own GPS map as an overlay to a useful background that you haven't had to compile and generate on your own.

Over the past few decades, our paper maps have been supplanted by digital map databases. We're all having to learn to think about mapping in new ways, and people differ on terminology. The background data I'll refer to here is nothing exotic. In fact my working definition of this kind of data says it must be "so broadly applicable and useful and have such a large return on investment that it should be made available as a public good (i.e., for free)."

Few GPS track logs make much sense outside of the context of some orienting background data. We can't really see where Hero the Dog has been just from his GPS track. In most cases the GPS track comes to life against an appropriately chosen background.

Finding the right GIS background theme for your GPS data is probably the most important, difficult, and frustrating task in this book.

Government at all levels spends billions of dollars on data. Like squirrels' winter food, there's lots of good GIS data hidden away on the Web, waiting for you to download or perhaps buy on CD. It's quite a trick to find the right background data. I'll give you some pointers on how to do this. But first, here's how to think and talk about various kinds of data that you should expect to be able to find for your GPS map.

A field guide to background data: "Vectors"...

A vector is a line that has a direction. "Vector data" is GIS jargon for data that's just lines, not an image. Shapefiles, for example, are vector data; they represent points, lines, or polygons. I hasten to explain that points are lines with zero length, and polygons are a bunch of lines strung together to surround an area such as a state or county.

The vector data I've used in *Fun with GPS* is very generic. In a perfect world, you would be able to get any of the vector data sets I describe for free or for the cost of making a copy.

Useful vector data includes boundaries of states, counties, towns, and land parcels. If you're lucky, your parcel data will come with building "footprints" (polygons showing the outline of buildings). The street and highway network is also a useful vector data set, as are shorelines and elevation contour lines.

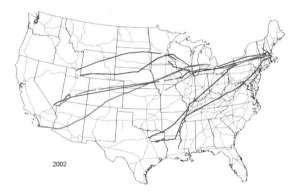

2002

State boundaries and highways

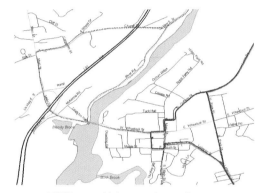

TIGER street, highway, and water features

Vector nautical chart

Parcel boundaries and building footprints: a "cadastral" map

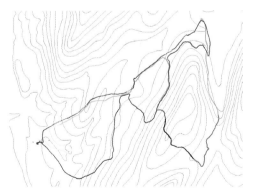

Vector contour lines

. . . and "rasters"

Raster data is another name for computerized images made up of rows of tiny dots. In the GPS/GIS world, these include images of paper maps such as topographic maps or nautical charts, as well as satellite or aerial photographs. The raster data sets I recommend have been specially processed so your mapping program will be able to overlay your GPS data in the right places. You may recognize that an aerial photo is in TIFF format, which you can view with your desktop darkroom program. But you'll notice that for mapping it will be paired with a TFW file, a "TIFF world file" that provides orientation and scaling information to the mapper.

Here's where the going gets complicated. Your GPS measures location in latitude and longitude. But none of these raster data sets is oriented to lat/long. They all use a projected coordinate system, either UTM (universal transverse Mercator) or a State Plane coordinate system specific to your state or sometimes part of a state.

Now you have to go back and reread all that gobbledygook about projections on page 12. Sorry 'bout that! It's difficult, but it's worth it.

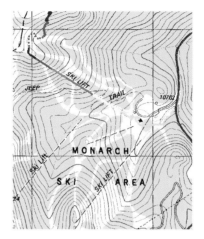

USGS digital raster graphics (DRG) image of topo map

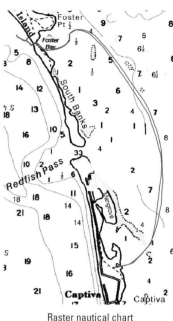

Raster nautical chart

USGS seamless aerial orthophoto

USGS digital Landsat mosaic (satellite imagery)

Digital orthophoto quad (DOQ) rectified aerial photo

Finding data: Portals and clearinghouses

Federal

Wouldn't it be nice if you could log onto a single, central Internet site, find exactly the background data set you need, and download it for free? That's the goal of several large and expensive efforts, some public and others private: to create a one-stop portal or clearinghouse for spatial data. One of these is *clearinghouse1.fgdc.gov*. Another is *www.geodata.gov/gos*.

You're paying for these federal portals and clearinghouses, so give them a try. Please describe your experiences with these sites on the Portal Survey page of *www.funwithgps.com*.

Private sector

A super ESRI-sponsored portal is *www.geographynetwork.com*. I found background data on this site for my friend Mike Smith (page 102) when he took one of my GPS units to Tasmania. This is also my preferred site for downloading TIGER street data in shapefile format.

Besides the portals just mentioned, a great site for public data is *nationalatlas.gov/atlasftp.html*. This site has some useful background layers such as state and county boundaries. You can download these as compressed shapefiles for ArcExplorer or ArcView. You'll have to decompress them before you can map them. Read the National Atlas FAQ first; it's about three-quarters of the way down the list of data layers. There's a lot more wonderful data on this site. I bet you can't resist downloading and mapping some of these, ranging from seismic hazards to crimes to zebra mussel infestations. Thank you, USGS!

Here are some other invaluable links:

- Stephan Pollard is on the second edition of this great site for finding data: *libinfo.uark.edu/GIS/us.asp*. Give it a try. Thanks, Stephan!

- Roelof Oddens maintains the granddaddy site for maps and spatial data, again at least a second edition, at *oddens.geog .uu.nl/index.php*. Thanks, Roelof!

- Joe Kerski leads the USGS effort for GIS in education. See *rockyweb.cr.usgs.gov/outreach/index.html*. If you click on Digital Geographic Data Resources and then Data Sites, you come to *rockyweb.cr.usgs.gov/outreach/rockylink_data.html*, which lists about two hundred links to sites supplying data you may want to use. Thanks, Joe!

Street centerlines

The street centerline data set is what you see when you look up an address or calculate a route using MapQuest® or Yahoo!® Maps. Both of these services use private-sector data sets. The pedigree of some of the private street data goes back to a public-domain centerline data set called TIGER, a product of the 1990 census, now moving into continuous update and maintenance. I had the good fortune to be involved in making the very first street centerline files back in 1967.

You may find you'll want to spend some money on a private data set. You can find out by trying the free TIGER coverage and seeing if it works for you.

You can learn more about TIGER at the Census Bureau Geography Division site at *www.census.gov/geo/www/tiger/index.html*. You can also download TIGER files, county by county, but I don't advise doing this because they arrive in a text format that must be converted to shapefiles before you can map them.

Instead, go to *www.geographynetwork.com* and find the Featured Content heading, then the Data heading under that. Click the Census TIGER/2000 link under the Data heading.

You'll traverse a bunch of screens to a choice of downloading by county or by data layer. I suggest that you pick a small nearby county and download all layers.

Your county will arrive zipped up, and when you go to unzip it, you will see that there are lots of layers! Print the *readme.html* file as a guide to the layers; you'll probably find that you can ignore most of the layers.

Start by unzipping the *lkA, lkH, lpy,* and *wat* files, representing roads, streams, landmarks, and lakes, respectively. You'll get four shapefiles to bring into ArcExplorer or ArcView. Remember to move the polygon themes to the bottom of the table of contents, so they'll plot first, and give them appropriate colors. I just did this for my county, and noticed that landmarks *(lpy)* include parks, airports, and water bodies. We have two versions of water bodies; try moving the landmarks *(lpy)* below the lakes in the table of contents. This gives you a good way to color the water features a different shade than other landmarks.

Topo maps and aerials

The dear old topo maps are probably the most recognizable and widely used maps in the United States. These are the ones that John Wesley Powell designed, and which took over a century to complete. They make a great background for your GPS tracks of hiking, snowmobiling, and other outdoor activities.

All the topos have been scanned. The scanned topos are DRG (digital raster graphics) files; see *topomaps.usgs.gov/drg.* You'll quickly learn that the USGS seems ambivalent about distributing DRGs, perhaps because of various legacy relationships with partners and relationships with private-sector suppliers. You can follow links and find lists of private companies that will sell you DRG topos. You can also get the USGS to fill your order for $50 plus a dollar per quad map that you want.

Another option is to buy a commercial software product bundled with digital topos for your state. Check *www.maptech.com, www.delorme.com,* or *maps.nationalgeographic.com/topo.* The products described at these sites have GPS interfaces and include digital elevation models (DEMs) that let you compute trail profiles and line-of-site calculations. These products are designed as complete solutions and you probably won't be able to export their topo maps in a form that ArcView or ArcExplorer can ingest. Search the three sites mentioned above to see if there are extensions to do this.

Along with DRGs, you've seen many examples using aerial photos as background wallpaper for GPS tracks. These are not just digital aerial photos; they've been orthorectified to make them look as if they were taken looking straight down at every point. Additionally, they are georeferenced so your mapping software can align them properly with your GPS tracks. These rectified, georeferenced aerial photos are often called digital orthophoto quads (DOQs) or simply digital orthophotos.

If you're on a limited budget, you'll probably share my feeling that resources like digital topo maps and aerials should be available as a public good. After all, we paid for them through state or federal taxes.

I've found free DRGs and DOQs for just about every project I wanted them for: heliskiing in Utah, the canoe race in Maine, backcountry skiing in Colorado, the skiing fund-raiser in New Hampshire. I just assume there's a state GIS agency with a download site.

You can find your state's GIS agency by searching the Web or by visiting *www.nsgic.org,* the National States Geographic Information Council's site. Click the States in Review link to go to State Profiles, then scroll down to your state. For my home state of New Hampshire, I find out about Fay Rubin's GRANIT organization in the first paragraph of an eight-page profile. Now back to the search engine, where I enter "granit gis." The first link takes me to the right site. (You may have to enter "granit gis data download" or whatever is appropriate for your state.)

Once on the GRANIT site, I click the GRANIT Data button. On the GRANIT Data page, Access the Database and Data Catalog links offer a couple of different ways to find and download what I want. Clicking the Data Catalog link takes me to an Alphabetical Listing of Layer Names link. In that list, I find a Digital Raster Graphics (DRGs) link. Clicking that calls up a status map showing that all quads are available. I then click Access the Database, click the By Town button, click Lyme in the resulting list, and am taken to a page that lets me download thirty-two data sets, including the DRGs and DOQs I need. Thanks, Fay!

Some state GIS agencies charge for large data sets. I've bought CDs of Vermont orthophotos for about 40 miles along the Connecticut River, many gigabytes of data. Harry Roush, who runs the Vermont Department of Taxes Mapping Program, charges a reasonable cost-of-copying fee to fill orders. This is only fair, I feel, especially as the department places no restrictions on further distribution of the data. Thanks, Harry!

Keep these state GIS agencies in mind if you appreciate the great services they provide. They're often threatened by budget cuts, and citizen support can go a long way.

Nautical charts

If you're reading this section, you know something about nautical charts. They usually depict a useful piece of geography ranging from a harbor approach to the entire New England coast. They will be at an appropriate scale to yield a manageable paper chart. Each chart will have a five-digit chart number.

Start at *nauticalcharts.noaa.gov/csdl/ctp/cm_vs.htm*. Click the Download button to see a form to narrow the search for your chart. If you know your chart number, you're home free; otherwise, enter a state name (e.g., Maine) in the state field to get a more manageable list of choices. To preview most of the charts, click the blue "Available" text.

You can download two very different kinds of charts from this page. Simplest, most complete, and most usable is the EVS Download. If this is available for the chart you want, give it a click, specify where you want the downloaded file to go, and unzip it. You'll find two shapefiles that, unlike the preview, only depict shorelines and navigable waters. Pretty slim pickin's. The good news, however, is that the shapefiles are in latitude and longitude, and matching them to the GPS track of your fishing trip or kayak expedition will be easy.

Next, click CM Download and download and unzip this version of your chart. Open a new view in ArcView or in a new ArcExplorer session and take a look. This is a raster image, with much more information: place-names, soundings, and so on. Basically it's a nautical chart with the navigational aids removed. But there's a huge obstacle to overlaying your GPS track, since every nautical chart is projected to its own unique Mercator projection.

Remember that you can't change the projection of a raster map; you have to make a projected version of your GPS track. You can't do this (a custom Mercator projection) in DNR Garmin, so this is going to be frustrating for ArcExplorer users. You can do a custom Mercator projection in ArcView. Hint: you need to know the "Latitude of true scale," which you can discover by opening your chart's .tfw file with a text processor such as Microsoft Word. A how-to page at *www.funwithgps.com* steps you through this process.

Don't use these databases for navigation! NOAA is in the process of implementing the next generation of digital nautical charts. See *nauticalcharts.noaa.gov/mcd/enc/index.htm*. Read about these, then try the download button and use the graphical or tabular search to see if your chart is available. You may be in luck. Otherwise, download any chart and check it out. You'll get a lot of shapefiles. There's no shortage of data in the ENCs! Thank you, NOAA!

A note about the future

Is GPS as we know it in 2005 as good as it gets? No way; it'll keep getting better, for several reasons: First, the federal government plans to keep upgrading the GPS ground- and space-based components of the system. One improvement scheduled within a decade is a civilian "L2" channel. This means another set of signals, at a different frequency, which will allow GPS receivers to more accurately reduce the impact of ionospheric vagaries on position accuracy. Also, planned replacement satellites will transmit a more powerful signal, meaning better reception for us, especially in marginal conditions.

Second, new technology keeps appearing. If you delve into the realm of GPS signal processing, you find that an enormous amount of processing goes into picking extremely faint GPS signals out of the background electronic noise, which the signals are designed to emulate. One approach is to put many processors on a chip, all instructed to listen for GPS signals. The net result is that the GPS receiver is much more likely to acquire a weak signal, simply because it takes less time. Inside a building, a signal may be barely strong enough to use for a few seconds. If a single processor is searching for it, the opportunity will probably pass. If there are a bunch of eager processors at work, one is likely to pick it up. To the user it'll just look as if your GPS now works indoors!

Finally, even though there are millions of consumer GPS units out in the world, the really big market is just emerging: cell phones. Last summer (2004) I started to see ads for cell phones with GPS. Interestingly, they're not touting the obvious safety implications (what we call "911 Phase II wireless ALI," or Automatic Location Identification), but consumer benefits: voice driving or walking directions. For a peek at where this is going, see *www.trimbleoutdoors.com*. Though Trimble Outdoors doesn't yet allow you to download and map track logs as I've described in this book, this is technically possible and may become a standard feature someday. All of this drives awareness and production up, costs down; this has gotta be good for *Fun* enthusiasts!

GPS Web sites

www.trimble.com/gps
The classic tutorial on how GPS works.

www.colorado.edu/geography/gcraft/notes/gps/gps_f.html
Another good tutorial. Lots of techie detail.

oceanservice.noaa.gov/education/geodesy/welcome.html
How GPS fits into the larger world of latitude and longitude.

gpsinformation.net
The granddaddy private GPS site. Check dates on material; some is old. Thanks, Joe, Jack, and Dale!

www.directionsmag.com/blog
If you only have time to read one source on GPS/GIS news, this is it. Thanks, Adena!

www.gpsdrawing.com/info.htm
GPS tracks as an art form? Elegant, restrained graphics; don't miss the sailplane graphics at the bottom of this page:
www.gpsdrawing.com/gallery/contributions/gliderashburn.htm
Also see the heart-rate graphics at:
www.gpsdrawing.com/gallery/contributions/hrgps.htm

www.geocomm.com/channel/gps/software
More GPS-related software, much free or inexpensive.

www.leapsecond.com/java/gpsclock.htm
GPS is based on time. This site will get you started on this subject.

www.kh-gps.de
"Auf Deutsch"; good perspectives and links.

www.monitoringtimes.com/html/gps.pdf
Good article for educators. Author Anton Ninno runs a Yahoo group (GPS-Mapping) for teachers using GPS.

www.knmi.nl/cliwoc
Pre-GPS tracking—a great project.

www.gpss.co.uk/bottle.htm
If this isn't fun with GPS, I don't know what is!

www.inertia-llc.com/sandbox/topofusiontest/index.html
Nice combination of GPS/GIS/digital photography.

www.shibumi.org/eoti.htm
The end.

Accuracy

Under good conditions*, your GPS will calculate coordinates with 3-meter accuracy. You can measure this yourself; I'll show you how. But first, what does 3-meter accuracy mean?

For measuring accuracy, I use a procedure adopted by the U.S. government about five years ago called the National Standard for Spatial Data Accuracy** (NSSDA). This involves running some simple statistics on a set of GPS readings taken at a known point. The result of the NSSDA procedure is the accuracy figure—say 3 meters—which means that 95 percent of the time your GPS coordinate measurements will be within 3 meters of "truth." This also means that, 5 percent of the time, your measurement will be more than 3 meters away from "truth." And the mean thing is that even if you do everything right, you never know which point is one of the good readings and which is in the delinquent 5 percent.

To test accuracy, the first thing you need to do is find a "true" location. To be a valid accuracy test, this point should have "the highest accuracy feasible." I use the National Geodetic Survey control points for testing GPS accuracy. You've probably seen these on mountaintops when you've been hiking. There are plenty down in the flat also; you shouldn't need to hike too far to find one. You can find the nearest control points by entering your coordinates in a form on the NGS site *(www.ngs.noaa.gov/cgi-bin/ds_radius.prl)*.

In the Data Type Desired scrolling list, choose Any Horizontal Control; many of these "brass caps" are elevation markers and won't give you a useful horizontal latitude/longitude reference. Try a search, perhaps increasing the search radius to get more possibilities. When you get one or more sites, select them and click Get Datasheets.

NGS data sheets aren't the snappiest travelogs you've ever read, though some of them do sport photos nowadays. Scroll down to the STATION DESCRIPTION section (all caps) and see if you recognize where it is and if you can get to it easily. Avoid stations on active runways and railroad trestles, for example. Print out the data sheet for your choice; the main thing you'll need will be the NAD 83 coordinates up near the top under "*CURRENT SURVEY CONTROL."

Station coordinates are in degrees, minutes, and seconds; convert them to decimal degrees using this formula:

$$\text{decimal degrees} = \text{degrees} + \text{minutes}/60 + \text{seconds}/3{,}600$$

Now you need to go out to the station and collect about thirty GPS readings. I suppose you could warm up your GPS and log thirty seconds of active track and call it a day. Would this give you a valid accuracy figure? Would it be the same if you came back and did the same thing six hours later? Instead, you could log one point per minute for thirty minutes. Or one point every ten minutes for five hours. There's no right answer; see how far you want to take this exercise and try various settings.

---

* Good conditions: WAAS enabled, open sky, black bars with "D"s (ephemeris and WAAS corrections for all satellites). The more satellites the better, especially if they are spread out across the sky.

** *www.fgdc.gov/standards/documents/standards/accuracy/chapter3.pdf*

Next, move your test points to the computer as a text file and open this file in Microsoft Excel. Copy the approximately thirty points you want to use into a new spreadsheet. You're going to calculate the root-mean-square of their deviation from the "true" value.

	Lat/longs of my test readings		Lat/longs of NGS station		Latitude difference: = F2 − C2	Longitude difference: = G2 − D2	Latitude difference, meters: = H2 * 111072	Longitude difference, meters: = I2 * 111072 * cos(43.65 * PI()/180)	Latitude and longitude differences, squared: = K2 * K2	= L2 * L2		Sum of squares: = M2 + N2	
	C	D	F	G	H	I	K	L	M	N	O	P	Q
1	Latitude	Longitude	Lat-Control	Long-Control	dLat, deg	dLong,deg	dLat,meters	dLong,meters	dLat squared	dLong, squared		sum of squares	
2	43.649860	-72.174220	43.6498389	-72.1742159	-0.0000211	0.0000042	-2.3391763	0.339170	5.47174586	0.11503618		5.587	
3	43.649852	-72.174218	43.6498389	-72.1742159	-0.0000128	0.0000024	-1.4172787	0.196108	2.00867897	0.03845822		2.047	
4	43.649847	-72.174223	43.6498389	-72.1742159	-0.0000077	0.0000075	-0.853033	0.601183	0.72766523	0.36142047		1.089	

(There are 37 points in this test.)

36	43.649837	-72.174222	43.6498389	-72.1742159	0.0000023	0.0000059	0.257687	0.475802	0.06640261	0.22638777		0.293	
37	43.649837	-72.174220	43.6498389	-72.1742159	0.0000024	0.0000042	0.2621299	0.333544	0.06871209	0.11125147		0.180	
38	43.649843	-72.174223	43.6498389	-72.1742159	-0.0000044	0.0000074	-0.492049	0.597164	0.24211218	0.35660480		0.599	
39												76.891	
40	Degree of Lat, meters: 111072											2.136	
41	Degree of Long, meters at 43.65N: 80372										RMSE	1.461	
42											ACCURACY	2.529	
43													

At the bottom of the spreadsheet, you calculate RMSE and accuracy.

Add the sums-of-squares: = sum (P2:P38)

Divide by one less than number of points: = P39/36

Take the square root to get RMSE: = sqrt (P40)

Multiply by fudge factor to get accuracy: = P41 * 2.4477/SQRT(2)

Accuracy and RMSE are in meters.

Most of this will look familiar if you've worked with statistics. There are two unusual issues to deal with. The first is translating from latitude and longitude coordinate differences to meters. This is simple for latitude, because each degree is a little more than 111,000 meters. Longitude difference is tricky, because meridians of longitude get closer together as you go north. A degree of longitude is about 111,000 meters at the equator, but it narrows to zero at the North Pole. You have to multiply by the cosine of the latitude to take this into account. Microsoft Excel further complicates this by needing angles expressed in radians, not degrees!

The second issue has to do with translating RMSE into a 95-percent-accuracy statistic. Since we're working in two dimensions, the multiplier to achieve this may not be familiar. See the FGDC document cited on page 123.

An experiment I would like to try is to get a good accuracy measurement, perhaps with thirty points at a point per minute, then rig up some way—maybe a square foot of aluminum foil attached to cardboard—to shield half the sky, and remeasure accuracy with another thirty points. I would expect the accuracy number to be larger; try it!

Speed calculations

Back in chapter 1, I introduced the idea of using a GPS as a speedometer. When your GPS calculates its position, it has to compute the Doppler shift of the signal from each satellite. Doppler shift is the apparent shifting of frequency of light or sound caused by the source moving toward or away from you. What matters to us is that your GPS knows the precise speed of each satellite relative to you; I guess it's just a matter of fancy computation to resolve all of these Doppler vectors into the speed and direction of your GPS relative to the surface of the earth.

This Doppler speed calculation is what your GPS displays. When a Magellan GPS stores a point, it stores Doppler speed along with lat, long, elevation, and time. This isn't the case with Garmin units; somebody made a decision not to store speed in the track log. However, we can calculate speed from consecutive coordinate readings. Here's how.

All the information you need is in the .dbf part of the shapefile created by DNR Garmin. Editing .dbf files in Microsoft Excel is perilous, and I needed adult assistance to succeed (thanks, Erik and Jesse!). For this example, let's say the track log was collected at one point per second and DNR Garmin was configured to generate projected coordinates in meters.

The projected coordinates are really useful for computing speed. Here's how to think about them: The y-projected field measures position in an up-down direction on the map; the x-projection measures position left to right across the map. If the x-projected value is 3 meters greater than it was the previous second, you've moved 3 meters across the map. If the y-projected value is 4 meters different from the previous reading, you've moved 4 meters in the up-down direction. Remember the "3-4-5 right triangle"? During this second, you've moved 5 meters diagonally. And, in order to do that, you had to be moving at 5 meters per second. This translates to 16.4 feet per second or 11.2 miles per hour.

Since you can't count on getting a 3-4-5 triangle every second, you have to use the more general formula for the hypotenuse of a right triangle to figure distance traveled:

hypotenuse = square root of the sum of the squares of the sides

Here's what this looks like in Excel:

	A	B	C	D	E	F	G	H	I	J	K	L	M	N
1	TYPE	IDENT	LAT	LONG	Y_PROJ	X_PROJ	NEW_SEG	ALTITUDE	TIME	y-dif	x-dif	m/sec	ft/sec	mph
2	TRACK	ACTIVE LOG	43.3912923	-72.3509322	99022.381	512077.286	False	554.00	2004/05/07-23:31:16					
3	TRACK	ACTIVE LOG	43.3912980	-72.3509342	99023.024	512077.121	False	554.00	2004/05/07-23:31:17	0.643	-0.165	0.664	2.178	1.485
4	TRACK	ACTIVE LOG	43.3913136	-72.3509415	99024.755	512076.527	False	554.00	2004/05/07-23:31:18	1.731	-0.594	1.830	6.004	4.093
5	TRACK	ACTIVE LOG	43.3913409	-72.3509612	99027.778	512074.926	False	552.00	2004/05/07-23:31:19	3.023	-1.601	3.421	11.225	7.653
6	TRACK	ACTIVE LOG	43.3913797	-72.3509911	99032.086	512072.494	False	552.00	2004/05/07-23:31:20	4.307	-2.432	4.946	16.228	11.064
7	TRACK	ACTIVE LOG	43.3914304	-72.3510364	99037.713	512068.817	False	551.00	2004/05/07-23:31:21	5.627	-3.677	6.722	22.053	15.036
8	TRACK	ACTIVE LOG	43.3914881	-72.3510953	99044.110	512064.031	False	548.00	2004/05/07-23:31:22	6.397	-4.786	7.989	26.211	17.871

For clarity, I label five new columns using some dBASE® naming rules: ten characters only; start with a letter.

I type formulas into cells J3 , K3 , L3 , M3 , and N3 : =E3–E2   =F3–F2   =sqrt(J3*J3+K3*K3)   =L3*3.2808   =M3*0.6818

Do you see how this calculates the speed in mph?

Once I've typed in these five formulas, I select (highlight) cells J3–N3 and drag these down to the last row. Now, pressing Ctrl + D propagates the formulas down to give you instantaneous mph for each second in the track log.

Now I have to do something totally weird and superstitious: click "Insert/name/define" to open a new window, then click "database". Down at the bottom of the window, you'll see that this "Refers to" spreadsheet cells A1 through I4532. But my edits added five more columns, so I have to change "I4532" to "N4532".

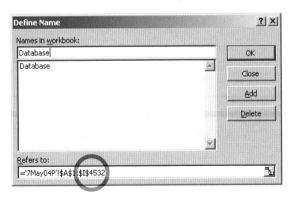

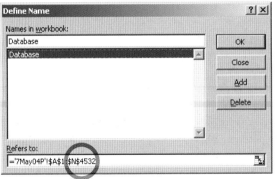

The red circles show where "I4532" is changed to "N4532."

Useful numbers   1 meter = 3.2808 feet   1 foot per second = .6818 miles per hour

Next, click OK and save the spreadsheet as an Excel file. Having done this, I save it once again as a dBASE IV file. Excel warns me that I'm about to replace the original .dbf file, which is all right, because (of course) I've made a backup copy of the shapefile before embarking on this exercise.

I sometimes make up a new file name—perhaps with a "-s" suffix (for speed)—rather than overwrite the original .dbf file. Remember that you will also have to copy and rename the .shp and .shx files.

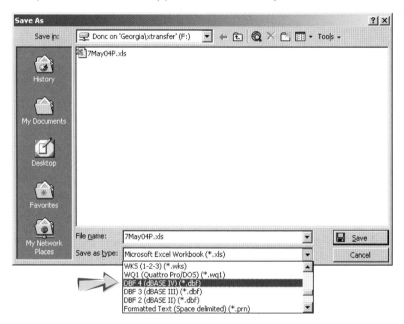

If I had been logging a point every three seconds, I would need to divide the result in L3 by three.

Occasionally your GPS will fail to record a track point for some given second. In this case you'll get a speed that's about twice what it should be. Scan the mph field and see if this happens. You can get fancy and compute the time between every point, and divide the "L" calculation by this value. I did this once, but realized that if the GPS is operating under really poor conditions, losing and regaining lock, the track point locations are going to be subject to all sorts of gremlins, and speeds calculated from these points are going to be of questionable value.

Finally, here's another example from a skydiver, where horizontal, vertical, and 3-D speed are all important. Altitude change is simple to compute: it's the current altitude subtracted from the altitude one second ago. At one point per second, altitude difference in feet is also vertical speed in feet per second. Excel computes this in column $\boxed{O}$: $\boxed{\texttt{=H3-H2}}$

	A	B	C	D	E	F	G	H	I	J	K	L	M	N	O	P	Q
	TYPE	IDENT	LAT	LONG	Y_PROJ	X_PROJ	NEW_SEG	ALTITUDE	TIME	y-dif	x-dif	m/sec	horiz-fps	horiz-mph	dVert	3D-fps	3D-mph
	TRACK	ACTIVE LOG	42.5782442	-72.3124409	925615.729	133303.416	False	14196.00	2004/06/27-14:42:54								
	TRACK	ACTIVE LOG	42.5782442	-72.3126125	925615.864	133289.324	False	14168.00	2004/06/27-14:42:55	0.134	-14.092	14.092	46.235	31.523	28.000	54.052	36.853
	TRACK	ACTIVE LOG	42.5782228	-72.3127198	925613.564	133280.494	False	14130.00	2004/06/27-14:42:56	-2.300	-8.830	9.125	29.937	20.411	38.000	48.376	32.983
	TRACK	ACTIVE LOG	42.5782013	-72.3128057	925611.247	133273.425	False	14081.00	2004/06/27-14:42:57	-2.317	-7.069	7.439	24.404	16.639	49.000	54.741	37.322
	TRACK	ACTIVE LOG	42.5781798	-72.3128700	925608.915	133268.117	False	14020.00	2004/06/27-14:42:58	-2.332	-5.308	5.798	19.021	12.968	61.000	63.897	43.565

We have horizontal distance in feet in column M, so we compute 3-D speed (fps) in column $\boxed{P}$ and mph in column $\boxed{Q}$:
$\texttt{=sqrt(M3*M3+O3*O3)}$ $\boxed{\texttt{=P3*0.6818}}$

Coordinate truncation and speed

Remember Thea's skating track in chapter 3? And Mary's letter to Garmin in chapter 4? For the moment, we're stuck with truncation in track logs collected with Geko, eTrex, and Foretrex GPSs. Here's an example at a control station:

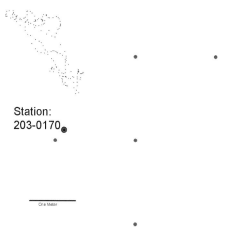

Station:
203-0170

One Meter

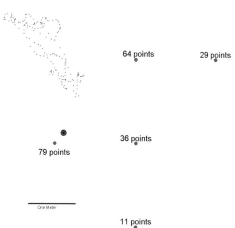

64 points

29 points

79 points

36 points

11 points

One Meter

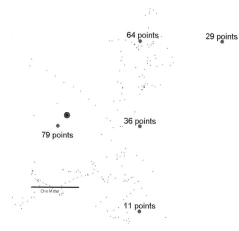

64 points

29 points

79 points

36 points

11 points

One Meter

1 I collect track logs with a Geko 201 and a Garmin 76 at a control station for a bit longer than three minutes. The Garmin 76 tracks (blue dots) jitter around over a couple of meters; the Geko tracks are snapped to one of five unique points.

2 Here's the same plot, with a count of track log readings at each of the five points.

3 Now a complication: At the same time I was collecting the track log, I was also logging the Geko readings to a laptop. These coordinate values (small red dots) aren't truncated!

4 I talk with a lot of GPS friends, including some very helpful folks at Garmin. Conclusions: Yes, the tracks downloaded by DNR Garmin are truncated, to .001 minute of arc. Yes, the Geko/eTrex/Foretrex GPS engines do compute coordinates to a finer precision. In fact, the internal track log is stored with more precision; we just can't download it. Why do I care about this? Because I like to be able to calculate speeds from the track log. See the example on the next page.

5 I drive along River Road in Lyme, north to south, as steadily as possible at about 10 mph, collecting track points with a Geko (blue, at the right) and a Garmin 76, each set to one point per second. Although the GPSs are next to each other on the dashboard, they plot about 3 meters apart, an acceptable variance.

6 The Garmin 76 records a smooth track. The Geko track exhibits truncation. All Geko points are snapped to the nearest .001 minute of latitude or longitude. This whole illustration is only about 80 meters north to south.

7 Same plot, annotated with distance in meters from previous point. Since the points are recorded one second apart, these distances also represent instantaneous speed in meters per second.

3.827	4.769
3.879	5.071 / 2.384
3.860	
3.803	4.769 / 2.383
3.806	
3.841	5.072 / 2.384
3.845	
3.827	4.768
3.809	5.071 / 2.383
3.804	
3.812	4.769 / 2.384
3.744	
3.734	5.071 / 2.384
3.807	
3.832	4.769
3.860	5.071 / 2.384
3.942	
4.045	4.768
4.196	5.072 / 2.384
4.220	

Speeds calculated from the Garmin 76's track vary by about 1 percent. Speeds from the Geko vary more than 100 percent.

Two days later I tested this with several other units at 10, 20, 30, 40, and 50 mph. As you might expect, the effect is proportionally smaller at higher speeds but still apparent even at 50 mph.

Do you see why the issue of coordinate truncation extends beyond the aesthetics of the track map of something that moves slowly over small distances? Not only does the mapped track look choppy, but speed calculations are practically useless. I happen to think that knowing instantaneous speed every second is really interesting and useful.

I like the Geko 201 as a data-collection device for GPS mapping. It works really well for skydivers, who tend to move pretty fast, especially in free fall. But truncation spoils Mary the Cat's

track map. And I'm not going to put her through another session with a Garmin 76. She's a good sport, but enough's enough!

For events like the polo game, where I'm really interested in both a good track and speed calculations, I'm going to continue to use Garmin 76s, external antennas, and lots of duct tape.

Garmin may or may not modify the software. It would be great if all GPSs would store Doppler speed for each track point. While I'm on the subject, it would be great if all GPSs would also store some accuracy indicators with each track point: Position Dilution of Precision (PDOP), number of satellites used, WAAS, and so on. Also, did that extrapolation algorithm have a say in the recorded coordinates?

I really wonder, when the product design folks put pen to paper (or whatever they do these days), if they know that their decisions affect the kind of *Fun* things you and I want to do with our GPSs? Speaking for myself, before I started this book, I had no idea that these units would work so well in so many different situations. Let's see what the future brings!

Back to what we have to work with today: remember when Tim Kelly set a personal best in the Boston Marathon? I really wanted to calculate his speeds over the 26-mile course. We had gone over the Geko-versus-GPSMAP 76 issues, and Tim balked at the size, weight, and complexity of using anything bigger than the Geko. I don't blame him; you can see the Geko rig we used on pages 58–59. So he pushed like crazy, generated a great track, and I really wanted to calculate his speed without that dumb jerkiness you see on the previous page.

I experimented with a moving average of speeds for each point. For example, I tried averaging the speed for the point with the speeds for the preceding and following points. It still came out choppy and unrealistic. I settled on a different kind of moving average: for each point I calculated the distance between the point 10 seconds ahead and the point 10 seconds back and divided by 20. This yielded usable speeds, which I used for mapping Tim's race.

Let's think about this technique. If you move at a constant velocity (speed and direction), it'll work fine. It clearly won't work for the first and last ten points in the track log, but we can live with that. If you change speeds a lot, this will dampen the effect of your acceleration. If you turn a sharp corner, you'll get distortions, as the distance calculation will "cut the corner" and give you a higher speed than actual. For Tim's marathon, there weren't many sharp turns, and acceleration is moderate for the most part, though I hasten to add that Tim can do wheelies with the racing chair. For contrast, consider polo ponies and their near-constant regime of speeding up, turning, and slowing down. This averaging method wouldn't work at all for them.

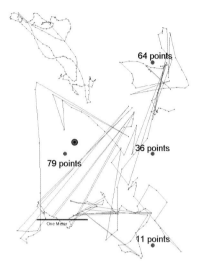

64 points

29 points

36 points

79 points

One Meter

11 points

When I got to this point I was nearing the end of April and still had lots of events on the list, so I moved on. There's plenty of room for people to pick up this subject and do a more thorough job. Please keep me posted on your work on calculating speed from truncated coordinates.

Finally, a postscript to Mary's request that Garmin change software. Long after I helped her draft her letter, I revisited my work plotted on the preceding page. I had discovered the neat conversion feature in DNR Garmin that allows you to make a line shapefile out of points that have a time stamp. I did this for the three minutes of Geko data I had logged to my laptop, and plotted the map above. Uh-oh. Though it's true that there's more coordinate granularity available within the Geko, that's not the whole story. See how the Garmin 76 track drifts around continuously? But the new line file shows that the Geko track is much more discontinuous. This could be due to the Geko GPS engine, the fact that the Geko's "patch" antenna doesn't work as well as the Garmin 76 model's quad-filar version, or that the Kalman filters are set differently in the two GPSs, or . . . something I just don't know about yet. Getting access to raw, active track log readings may be only part of the solution Mary wants. There's always something new to learn.

Accuracy of speed calculations

When we take a GPS to a control station and follow the NSSDA procedures, we find that a consumer GPS with WAAS will measure location with an accuracy around 3 meters. Ninety-five percent of lat/long readings will be within 3 meters of the "true" value, and one out of twenty might be somewhat farther away. I've used this procedure a lot; I can drive to several local control stations as easily as I can get to our favorite pizza place. But when I mailed Sean's ice-race map to him, I realized that I had no idea at all about the accuracy of the instantaneous speeds I plotted on each track point along his drive.

Various Web searches on GPS speed accuracy clued me in as to how GPSs calculate speed (see the Doppler stuff a few pages back). But that wasn't what I was doing. I was just calculating the distance the GPS had traveled since the last track point and dividing by the time interval between readings. How accurate are speeds measured this way?

I got to thinking about this and asked some friends. In my most common case where I'm logging one track point per second, the lat/long accuracy of each point is important, as is the assumption that the GPS is calculating positions precisely every second. We also have to remember that our calculated speed assumes the GPS moved directly from one track point to the next, which we've noticed isn't the case all the time. Recall how Bucky's car 26 travels in an arc between track points and actually moves farther and faster than the straight-line distance and computed speed.

I have to assume that the GPS times are spot-on. I see no evidence that they aren't, and I've been too busy chasing athletes and animals around with my duct tape and GPS gear to research this in depth. So any error in calculating GPS speeds must come from errors in the lat/long readings.

You may be thinking, "That's simple; we know the accuracy of these readings. It's around 3 meters." Yes . . . but if that were all there was to it, we wouldn't see the calculated speeds coming out as well as they do.

In fact, the speed calculation formula really doesn't care at all about the "absolute" accuracy of the GPS reading. I kept turning this over in my mind and gradually it became apparent that accuracy of the instantaneous speed calculations must be related to the second-by-second drift of GPS readings that you see at a fixed location. I've observed and recorded this a lot; see the plot of three minutes of Garmin 76 readings on the previous two pages. It's quite rare to see a fully warmed-up stationary GPS drifting more than a few inches from second to second.

So here's what some smart person has to do: record a bunch of track points at a stationary location, analyze their second-to-second positions to get a model of drift, then calculate how this drift—in various directions and for both endpoints—will affect calculated distance (hence speed). The faster the GPS moves, the better the accuracy should be, as the second-by-second drift will get smaller in comparison to the distance between the points.

I was still puzzling over whether this model—based on a stationary GPS—was valid for the case of a moving one. I e-mailed Ken Milnes, who had worked on GPSing all of the NASCAR racers for SporTVision. Ken reminded me that my "stationary" GPS isn't stationary at all; it's located on the surface of a rotating planet! In fact, at the equator a "stationary" GPS is moving 1,000 miles per hour. "Absolute" location is a parochial idea; all motion—and position—is relative. So this approach is valid; somebody please work through it and let me know how it comes out.

GPS gremlins

Under good conditions, your GPS tracks are going to be good, but not perfect. Under not-so-good conditions, GPS tracks can look pretty perplexing. Here's a recapitulation of several GPS gremlins we've encountered throughout the book:

1 *The rude awakening.* You turn on the GPS and stride out into the woods. At first the GPS doesn't record any points; it doesn't have ephemeris information for any satellites. As soon as it acquires ephemerides for three satellites, it will announce a 2-D fix and start storing track points. Recall that a 2-D fix isn't just a good lat/long reading with no elevation information; it's a lat/long estimate based on guessing at the elevation. Not very accurate. When a fourth satellite kicks in, you'll get a 3-D fix, probably with more accurate lat/longs. When you look at the track log, you may be able to tell when this happened, because the elevation value will suddenly jump and start to fluctuate. The lat/long will probably jump also. As the GPS acquires more and more ephemerides, the lat/long values will get more and more accurate, probably with a jump as each new satellite is used in the solution. At some point WAAS information will become available, satellite by satellite, and there may be further positional jumps as the fix is refined. I suppose you could run a controlled experiment to demonstrate this if you had a nearby straight railroad track running through the woods.

2 *Abrupt loss of signal.* Your GPS is doing fine; you see black bars and "D"s. Then you drive under a bridge, walk indoors, or just cover the antenna. The Garmin extrapolation algorithm cuts in and starts creating a string of up to thirty fictitious points in the same direction and spacing of the last real observations.

3 *Partial loss of signal.* Your view of the sky is partially blocked; you drive between tall buildings or walk up to a structure and lose half the sky. You may still have enough satellites for a 2-D or even 3-D fix, but they won't be evenly spread out and your fix will suffer from increased Position Dilution of Precision (PDOP). Your fix will suffer and the track log will probably record a jump.

4 *Partial, then total, loss of signal.* Oh, this one's nasty: you lose most of your satellites and your fix jumps. Then the next second you drop to two or fewer satellites and the GPS can't compute a fix. What happens? The extrapolation algorithm kicks in, but now it's extrapolating from that last fix, which had jumped due to reduced accuracy. Now the extrapolated track takes off for up to thirty seconds at an anomalous speed or direction or both.

5 *Multipath.* Direct line of sight is blocked to one or more satellites, but the receiver picks up signals reflected off buildings or a snow field. That signal will have traveled farther than the direct one and will make the position jump if it's used in the position solution. Though I mention this in the heliskiing section, you're not going to see this as often as other gremlins.

6 *Recovery of signal.* That's good, isn't it: to get the satellites back after you've lost them? Sure, but as they're used for the position solution, you're subject to seeing position shifts as accuracy improves. Your track log won't tell you this is happening; you'll have to deduce it from plotting the points. Remember Iver's track on the ski lift? He's going straight as an arrow, but the lift goes up steep terrain and in and out of tree cover. You can see him wander off track a bit, then the track takes a big jump and slowly eases back to the lift line. I really don't know why the track doesn't just pop back into place. Maybe those mysterious Kalman filters are at work. Let me know if you can explain these tracks.

Books from *ESRI Press*

Continued on next page

When ordering, please mention book title and ISBN (number that follows each title)

Books from ESRI Press (continued)

Planning Support Systems: Integrating Geographic Information Systems, Models, and Visualization Tools *1-58948-011-2*

Remote Sensing for GIS Managers *1-58948-081-3*

Salton Sea Atlas *1-58948-043-0*

Spatial Portals: Gateways to Geographic Information *1-58948-131-3*

The ESRI Guide to GIS Analysis, Volume 1: Geographic Patterns and Relationships *1-879102-06-4*

The ESRI Guide to GIS Analysis, Volume 2: Spatial Measurements and Statistics *1-58948-116-X*

Think Globally, Act Regionally: GIS and Data Visualization for Social Science and Public Policy Research *1-58948-124-0*

Thinking About GIS: Geographic Information System Planning for Managers (paperback edition) *1-58948-119-4*

Transportation GIS *1-879102-47-1*

Undersea with GIS *1-58948-016-3*

Unlocking the Census with GIS *1-58948-113-5*

Zeroing In: Geographic Information Systems at Work in the Community *1-879102-50-1*

Forthcoming titles from ESRI Press

Arc Hydro: GIS for Water Resources, Second Edition *1-58948-126-7*

A to Z GIS: An Illustrated Dictionary of Geographic Information Systems *1-58948-140-2*

Charting the Unknown: How Computer Mapping at Harvard Became GIS *1-58948-118-6*

Finding Your Customers: GIS for Retail Management *1-58948-123-2*

GIS for Environmental Management *1-58948-142-9*

GIS for the Urban Environment *1-58948-082-1*

GIS Methods for Urban Analysis *1-58948-143-7*

The GIS Guide for Local Government Officials *1-58948-141-0*

Ask for ESRI Press titles at your local bookstore or order by calling 1-800-447-9778. You can also shop online at www.esri.com/esripress. Outside the United States, contact your local ESRI distributor.

ESRI Press titles are distributed to the trade by the following:

In North America, South America, Asia, and Australia:
Independent Publishers Group (IPG)
Telephone (United States): 1-800-888-4741 • Telephone (international): 312-337-0747
E-mail: frontdesk@ipgbook.com

In the United Kingdom, Europe, and the Middle East:
Transatlantic Publishers Group Ltd.
Telephone: 44 20 8849 8013 • Fax: 44 20 8849 5556 • E-mail: transatlantic.publishers@regusnet.com

ESRI Press • 380 New York Street • Redlands, California 92373-8100 • www.esri.com/esripress